The Gilded Age
1877-1896

GOLDENTREE BIBLIOGRAPHIES
IN AMERICAN HISTORY

under the series editorship of
ARTHUR S. LINK

AMERICAN COLONIES IN THE EIGHTEENTH CENTURY, THE, 1689-1763 •
Jack P. Greene
AMERICAN COLONIES IN THE SEVENTEENTH CENTURY, THE • Alden T. Vaughan
AMERICAN ECONOMIC HISTORY BEFORE 1860 • George Rogers Taylor
AMERICAN ECONOMIC HISTORY SINCE 1860 • Edward C. Kirkland
AMERICAN REVOLUTION, THE • John Shy
AMERICAN SOCIAL HISTORY BEFORE 1860 • Gerald N. Grob
AMERICAN SOCIAL HISTORY SINCE 1860 • Robert H. Bremner
GILDED AGE, THE, 1877-1896 • Vincent P. De Santis
HISTORY OF AMERICAN EDUCATION, THE • Jurgen Herbst
MANIFEST DESTINY AND THE COMING OF THE CIVIL WAR, 1841-1860 •
Don E. Fehrenbacher
NATION IN CRISIS, THE, 1861-1877 • David Donald
PROGRESSIVE ERA AND THE GREAT WAR, THE, 1896-1920 • Arthur S. Link &
William M. Leary, Jr.
RELIGION IN AMERICAN LIFE • Nelson R. Burr

FORTHCOMING TITLES

AFRO-AMERICAN HISTORY
AMERICAN DIPLOMATIC HISTORY BEFORE 1890 • Norman A. Graebner
AMERICAN DIPLOMATIC HISTORY SINCE 1890 • W. B. Fowler
AMERICAN CONSTITUTIONAL DEVELOPMENT • Alpheus T. Mason
AMERICAN NATIONALISM AND SECTIONALISM, 1801-1841 • Edwin A. Miles
AMERICAN URBAN DEVELOPMENT • Seymour J. Mandelbaum
CONFEDERATION AND THE CONSTITUTION, THE, 1781-1801 • E. James Ferguson
FRONTIER AND THE AMERICAN WEST, THE • Rodman W. Paul
NEW SOUTH, THE • Paul M. Gaston
OLD SOUTH, THE • Fletcher M. Green

THE GILDED AGE
1877-1896

compiled by

Vincent P. DeSantis
University of Notre Dame

AHM PUBLISHING CORPORATION
Northbrook, Illinois 60062

ISBN: 0-88295-536-5

Library of Congress Card No.: 72-96558

PRINTED IN THE UNITED STATES OF AMERICA

733-1

To my students,
past and present,
in the Gilded Age,
University of Notre Dame

Editor's Foreword

are designed to provide students, teachers, and librarians with ready and reliable guides to the literature of American History in all its remarkable scope and variety. Volumes in the series cover comprehensively the major periods in American history, while additional volumes are devoted to all important subjects.

Goldentree Bibliographies attempt to steer a middle course between the brief list of references provided in the average textbook and the long bibliography in which significant items are often lost in the sheer number of titles listed. Each bibliography is, therefore, selective, with the sole criterion for choice being the significance—and not the age—of any particular work. The result is bibliographies of all works, including journal articles and doctoral dissertations, that are still useful, without bias in favor of any particular historiographical school.

Each compiler is a scholar long associated, both in research and teaching, with the period or subject of his volume. All compilers have not only striven to accomplish the objective of this series but have also cheerfully adhered to a general style and format. However, each compiler has been free to define his field, make his own selections, and work out internal organization as the unique demands of his period or subject have seemed to dictate.

The single great objective of *Goldentree Bibliographies in American History* will have been achieved if these volumes help researchers and students to find their way to the significant literature of American history.

Arthur S. Link

Preface

ANY BIBLIOGRAPHY THAT attempts to deal with the historical writing about the United States during any period is bound to be selective. This bibliography, covering the main developments in American history between 1877 and 1896, is no exception. Nevertheless, I have tried to include most of the significant books, articles, and dissertations on a variety of subjects of the Gilded Age, although I have no doubt that other scholars will dispute some of my choices. I invite suggestions for additions to future editions of this bibliography.

I hope the topical organization of this volume combined with cross-references will facilitate its use.

And I trust that readers will learn as much from using this bibliography as I learned in compiling it.

I should like to thank Margaret L. Lippert for typing the final manuscript and proofreading it.

Vincent P. de Santis

Abbreviations

Ag Hist	Agricultural History
Am Archiv	American Archives
Am Cath Hist Rev	American Catholic Historical Review
Am Econ Rev	American Economic Review
Am Hist Rev	American Historical Review
Am J Econ Socio	American Journal of Economics and Sociology
Am J Int Law	American Journal of International Law
Am J Legal Hist	American Journal of Legal History
Am J Pol	American Journal of Politics
Am Jew Hist Q	American Jewish History Quarterly
Am Jour Sociol	American Journal of Sociology
Am Law Rev	American Law Review
Am Mercury	American Mercury
Am Pol Sci Rev	American Political Science Review
Am Q	American Quarterly
Am Rev Rev	American Review of Reviews
Am Sch	American Scholar
Am West	The American West
Ann Am Acad	Annals of the American Academy
Ann Am Acad Pol Soc Sci	Annals, American Academy of Political and Social Science
Ann Med Hist	Annals of Medical History
Ann Rep Am Hist Assoc	Annual Report, American Historical Association
Ann Wyo	Annals of Wyoming
Ant Rev	Antioch Review
Ariz Hist Rev	Arizona Historical Review
Ark Hist Q	Arkansas Historical Quarterly
Atl Month	Atlantic Monthly
Bos Univ Law Rev	Boston University Law Review
Bull Dept Ag	Bulletin, Department of Agriculture
Bull Dept Labor	Bulletin Department of Labor
Bull Hist Med	Bulletin History of Medicine
Bus Hist Rev	Business History Review
Calif Hist Soc Q	California Historical Society Quarterly
Cent Illus Month Mag	Century Illustrated Monthly Magazine
Cent Mag	Century Magazine
Chron Okla	Chronicles of Oklahoma
Civil War Hist	Civil War History
Coll Kan State Hist Soc	Collections, Kansas State Historical Society

Coll Minneapolis Hist Soc	Collections, Minneapolis Historical Society
Colo Mag	Colorado Magazine
Colum Law Rev	Columbia Law Review
Cur Hist	Current History
Farmer's Bull Dept Ag	Farmer's Bulletin Department of Agriculture
Fortnightly Rev	Fortnightly Review
Ga Hist Q	Georgia Historical Quarterly
Har Law Rev	Harvard Law Review
Har Mag	Harper's Magazine
Har Week	Harper's Weekly
His-Am Hist Rev	Hispanic-American Historical Review
Hist	The Historian
Hist Mag	Historical Magazine
Hist Rec Stud (U S Cath Hist Soc)	Historical Records Studies, United States Catholic Historical Society
Hunt Lib Q	The Huntington Library Quarterly
Ill Law Rev	Illinois Law Review
Ill State Hist Soc J	Illinois State Historical Society Journal
Ind Mag Hist	Indiana Magazine of History
Int Rev Soc Hist	International Review of Social History
Iowa J Hist	Iowa Journal of History
Iowa J Hist Pol	Iowa Journal of History and Politics
J Am Hist	Journal of American History
J Am Stud	Journal of American Studies
J Ch State	Journal of Church and State
J Miss Hist	Journal of Mississippi History
J Econ Bus Hist	Journal of Economic and Business History
J Econ Hist	Journal of Economic History
J Ill State Hist Soc	Journal of Illinois State Historical Society
J Mod Hist	Journal of Modern History
J Neg Educ	Journal of Negro Education
J Neg Hist	The Journal of Negro History
J Pol	The Journal of Politics
J Pol Econ	Journal of Political Economy
J Rel	Journal of Religion
J S Hist	The Journal of Southern History
J Soc Sci	Journal of the Social Sciences
Jour Q	Journalism Quarterly
Kan Hist Q	Kansas Historical Quarterly
Kan Q	Kansas Quarterly
La Hist	Louisiana History
La Hist Q	The Louisiana Historical Quarterly
McClure's Mag	McClure's Magazine
Marx Q	The Marxist Quarterly
Mich Law Rev	Michigan Law Review
Mid Am	Mid-America
Minn Hist	Minnesota History

Minn Hist Bull	Minnesota History Bulletin
Miss Q	Mississippi Quarterly
Miss Val Hist Rev	The Mississippi Valley Historical Review
Mo Hist Rev	Missouri Historical Review
N Amer Rev	The North American Review
N C Hist Rev	North Carolina Historical Review
N C F	Nineteenth Century Fiction
N D Hist Q	North Dakota Historical Quarterly
N D Q	North Dakota Quarterly
N Eng Mag	New England Magazine
N Eng Q	New England Quarterly
N M Hist Rev	The New Mexico Historical Review
N Y Hist	New York History
N Y Hist Soc Q	New York Historical Society Quarterly
N Y Univ Law Q Rev	New York University Law Quarterly Review
Natl Hist	Natural History
Neb Hist	Nebraska History
Neb Hist Mag	Nebraska History Magazine
Nor-Am Stud Rec	Norwegian-American Studies and Records
Ohio Hist Q	The Ohio Historical Quarterly
Ohio State Arch Hist Q	Ohio State Archaeological and Historical Quarterly
Ore Hist Q	Oregon Historical Quarterly
Pa Hist	Pennsylvania History
Pa Mag Hist Biog	The Pennsylvania Magazine of History and Biography
Pac Hist Rev	Pacific Historical Review
Pac N W Q	The Pacific Northwest Quarterly
Pear Mag	Pearson's Magazine
Philos Sci	Philosophy of Science
Phylon	Phylon
Pol Sci Q	Political Science Quarterly
Proc Am Ant Soc	Proceedings, American Antiquarian Society
Proc Am Philos Soc	Proceedings, the American Philosophical Society
Proc Mass Hist Soc	Proceedings, Massachusetts Historical Society
Proc Miss Val Hist Assn	Proceedings, Mississippi Valley Historical Association
Proc U S Naval Inst	Proceedings, United States Naval Institute
Psych Bull	Psychological Bulletin
Pub Am Econ Assn	Publications of American Economic Association
Pub Am Stat Assn	Publications of American Statistical Association
Pub Hist (E Car Col)	Publications in History, East Carolina College
Q J Econ	Quarterly Journal of Economics
Q J Lib Cong	Quarterly Journal of the Library of Congress
Rep Am Bar Assn	Report of American Bar Association
Rep Bur Animal Indus	Report, Bureau of Animal Industry
Rep U S Comm Ed	Report, United States Commissioner of Education

Rev Econ Stat	Review of Economics and Statistics
Rev Pol	Review of Politics
Rev Rev	Review of Reviews
Sat Rev	Saturday Review
S Atl Q	South Atlantic Quarterly
S Calif Q	Southern California Quarterly
S C Hist Assn Proc	South Carolina Historical Association Proceedings
S C Hist Mag	South Carolina Historical Magazine
S D Hist Coll	South Dakota Historical Collections
S W Hist Q	Southwestern Historical Quarterly
S W Pol Sci Q	Southwestern Political Science Quarterly
S W Rev	Southwest Review
S W Soc Sci Q	Southwestern Social Science Quarterly
Sci	Science
Sci Soc	Science and Society
Scrib Mag	Scribner's Magazine
Soc Ed	Social Education
Soc Forces	Social Forces
Speech J	Speech Journal
Stan Law Rev	Stanford Law Review
Stud Hist (Smith)	Studies in History, Smith College
Stud Hist Econ Pub Law (Colum)	Studies in History, Economics, and Public Law (Columbia Studies in the Social Sciences)
Tex Law Rev	Texas Law Review
Tran Am Inst Min Engr	Transactions, American Institute of Mining Engineers
Tran Ill State Hist Soc	Transactions, Illinois State Historical Society
Tran Wis Acad	Transactions, the Wisconsin Academy
Univ N D Q J	University of North Dakota Quarterly Journal
Utah Hist Q	Utah Historical Quarterly
Va Mag Hist Biog	Virginia Magazine of History and Biography
Vt Hist	Vermont History
Wash Hist Q	Washington Historical Quarterly
W Hist Q	The Western Historical Quarterly
W Pa Hist Mag	Western Pennsylvania Historical Magazine
W Pol Q	Western Political Quarterly
Wis Hist Soc Proc	Wisconsin Historical Society Proceedings
Wis Mag Hist	Wisconsin Magazine of History
Yale Law J	Yale Law Journal
Yrbk Dept Ag	Yearbook, Department of Agriculture
Yrbk Swed Hist Soc Am	Yearbook, Swedish Historical Society of America
Yrbk W Tex Hist Assn	Yearbook, West Texas Historical Association

NOTE: *Cross-references are to item numbers. Items marked by a dagger (†) are available in paperback edition at the time this bibliography goes to press. The publisher and compiler invite suggestions for additions to future editions of the bibliography.*

Contents

I. Bibliographical Guides and Selected Reference Works

1 ADAMS, James T., et al., eds. *Dictionary of American History.* 6 vols., plus index. New York, 1940-1961.

2 American Historical Association. *Writings on American History.* 46 vols. Washington, D.C., 1902-1964.

3 BASLER, Roy P., et al., eds. *A Guide to the Study of the United States of America: Representative Books Reflecting the Development of American Thought and Life.* Washington, D.C., 1960.

4 BEERS, Henry P. *Bibliographies in American History: Guide to Materials for Research.* Rev. ed. New York, 1942.

5 BEMIS, Samuel Flagg, and Grace Gardner GRIFFIN, eds. *Guide to the Diplomatic History of the United States, 1775-1921.* Washington, D.C., 1935.

6 BOEHM, Eric, ed. *America: History and Life: A Guide to Periodical Literature.* Santa Barbara, Calif., 1964- .

7 BOYD, Annie M. *United States Government Publications.* 2d ed. New York, 1941.

8 Bureau of the Census. *Historical Statistics of the United States, Colonial Times to 1957.* Washington, D.C., 1960.

9 *Catalogue of Books Represented by Library of Congress Printed Cards.* 167 vols. Ann Arbor., 1942-1946. (This Library of Congress printed catalogue is a basic guide to books and pamphlets. It should be used in conjunction with the Supplement [42 vols. Ann Arbor, 1948], *The Library of Congress Author Catalogue* . . . 1948-1952 [24 vols. Ann Arbor, 1953], and *The National Union Catalog* [Ann Arbor, 1961-], which includes books published after 1952.)

10 *Checklist of United States Public Documents, 1789-1909.* Washington, D.C., 1911.

11 Congress of the United States. *Biographical Directory of the American Congress, 1774-1961.* Washington, D.C., 1961.

12 *Dissertation Abstracts: A Guide to Dissertations and Monographs Available in Microform.* Ann Arbor, 1938- . (Early volumes entitled *Microfilm Abstracts.*)

13 *Doctoral Dissertations Accepted by American Universities.* 22 vols. New York, 1934-1955.

14 ELLIS, John Tracy. *A Guide to American Catholic History.* Milwaukee, 1959.

15 *Essay and General Literature Index.* New York, 1934- .

16 HALE, Richard W., Jr., ed. *Guide to Photocopied Historical Materials in the United States and Canada.* Ithaca, N.Y., 1961.

1

17 HAMER, Philip M., ed. *A Guide to Archives and Manuscripts in the United States.* New Haven, 1961.

18 HANDLIN, Oscar, et al., eds. *The Harvard Guide to American History.* Cambridge, Mass., 1954.†

19 HIGHAM, John, ed. *The Reconstruction of American History.* New York, 1962.†

20 HOWE, George F., et al., eds. *The American Historical Association's Guide to Historical Literature.* New York, 1961.

21 *International Index to Periodicals.* New York, 1916- .

22 JOHNSON, Allen, and Dumas MALONE, eds. *Dictionary of American Biography.* 22 vols. New York, 1928-1958.

23 KAPLAN, Louis, ed. *A Bibliography of American Autobiographies.* Madison, 1961.

24 KUEHL, Warren F., ed. *Dissertations in History: An Index to Dissertations Completed in History Departments of United States and Canadian Universities, 1873-1960.* Lexington, Ky., 1965.

25 LARSON, Henrietta M. *Guide to Business History.* Cambridge, Mass., 1948.

26 MILLER, Elizabeth W., ed. *The Negro in America: A Bibliography.* Cambridge, Mass., 1966. 2d ed. Mary L. Fisher, comp. Cambridge, Mass., 1970.

27 MORRIS, Richard B., ed. *Encyclopedia of American History.* Rev. ed. New York, 1961.

28 National Research Council et al. *Doctoral Dissertations Accepted by American Universities. . . .* 22 vols. New York, 1933-1955.

29 *National Union Catalogue of Manuscript Collections.* 5 vols. to date, plus indexes. Ann Arbor, Hamden, Conn., and Washington, D.C., 1962- .

30 NEUFIELD, Maurice F. *A Representative Bibliography of American Labor History.* Ithaca, N.Y., 1964.†

31 *Nineteenth Century Readers' Guide to Periodical Literature. 1890-1899.* 2 vols. New York, 1944.

32 O'NEILL, Edward H. *Biography by Americans, 1658-1936: A Subject Bibliography.* Philadelphia, 1939.

33 PETERSON, Clarence Stewart. *Bibliography of County Histories of the 3,111 Counties in the United States.* 2d ed. Baltimore, 1946. Suppls. 1950, 1955, 1960.

34 POOLE, William F., et al., eds. *Poole's Index to Periodical Literature* [1802-1902]. 6 vols. Boston, 1882-1908.

35 POORE, Benjamin P. *A Descriptive Catalogue of the Government Publications of the United States,* September 5, 1775-March 4, 1881. Washington, D.C., 1885.

36 *Readers' Guide to Periodical Literature.* New York, 1900- .

37 SCHMECKEBIER, Laurence. *Government Publications and Their Use.* Washington, D.C., 1936.

38 SPILLER, Robert E., et al., eds. *Literary History of the United States.* Rev. ed. New York, 1963.

39 STROUD, Gene S., and Gilbert E. DONAHUE. *Labor History in the United States: A General Bibliography.* Urbana, Ill., 1961.

40 WINCHELL, Constance M. *Guide to Reference Books.* 8th ed. Chicago, 1967.

41 WOODRESS, James. *Dissertations in American Literature, 1891-1955*, with *Supplement, 1958-1961.* Durham, N.C., 1962.

II. General Statistical and Documentary Compilations

42 *American Annual Cyclopaedia and Register of Important Events.* 42 vols. New York, 1862-1903.

43 BAIN, Richard C. *Convention Decisions and Voting Records.* Washington, D.C., 1966.

44 BURNHAM, W. D. *Presidential Ballots, 1836-1892.* Baltimore, 1955.

45 *Congressional Record, Containing the Proceedings and Debates, 1873-* . Washington, D.C., 1873- .

46 *Historical Statistics of the United States: Colonial Times to 1957.* Washington, D.C., 1960.

47 *Journal of the Executive Proceedings of the Senate of the United States, 1789-1905.* 90 vols. Washington, D.C., 1828-1948.

48 *Journal of the House of Representatives of the United States.* Philadelphia and Washington, D.C., 1789- .

49 *Journal of the Senate of the United States.* Philadelphia and Washington, D.C., 1789- .

50 *Papers Relating to Foreign Relations* [of the United States]. Washington, D.C., 1861- .

51 PAULLIN, Charles O. *Atlas of the Historical Geography of the United States.* Ed. John K. Wright. Washington, D.C., 1932.

52 PORTER, Kirk H., and Donald B. JOHNSON, eds. *National Party Platforms, 1840-1956.* Urbana, Ill., 1956.

53 RICHARDSON, James D. *A Compilation of the Messages and Papers of the Presidents, 1789-1897.* 10 vols. Washington, D.C., 1907.

III. American Politics from Rutherford B. Hayes to Grover Cleveland, 1877–1897

1. General

54 ADAMS, Henry. *Democracy.* New York, 1880.†

55 ANDREWS, Elisha Benjamin. *The Last Quarter-Century in the United States: 1870–1895.* New York, 1896.

56 BINKLEY, Wilfred E. *American Political Parties: Their Natural History.* Rev. ed. New York, 1945.

57 BRYCE, James. *The American Commonwealth.* 2 vols. New York, 1888.†

58 BUCK, Paul H. *The Road to Reunion: 1865–1900.* Boston, 1937.†

59 DEGLER, Carl. "The Nineteenth Century." *Theory and Practice in American Politics.* Ed. William H. Nelson. Chicago, 1964.

60 DE SANTIS, Vincent P. "American Politics in the Gilded Age." *Rev Pol,* XXV (1963), 551–561.

61 DE SANTIS, Vincent P. "Republican Efforts to 'Crack' the Solid South." *Rev Pol,* XIV (1952), 244–264.

62 DE SANTIS, Vincent P. "The Republican Party Revisited, 1877–1897." *The Gilded Age, A Reappraisal.* Ed. H. Wayne Morgan. Syracuse, 1963.

63 DE SANTIS, Vincent P. *Republicans Face the Southern Question: The New Departure Years 1877–1897.* Baltimore, 1959.

64 EIDSON, William G. "Who Were the Stalwarts?" *Mid-Am,* LII (1970), 235–261.

65 FAULKNER, Harold U. *Politics, Reform and Expansion 1890–1900.* New York, 1959.†

66 FINE, Sidney. *Laissez-Faire and the General Welfare State: A Study of Conflict in American Thought, 1865–1901.* Ann Arbor, 1956.†

67 FORD, Henry Jones. *The Rise and Growth of American Politics: A Sketch of Constitutional Development.* New York, 1898.

68 GARRATY, John A. *The New Commonwealth, 1877–1890.* New York, 1968.†

69 GINGER, Ray. *Age of Excess: The United States from 1877 to 1914.* New York, 1965.†

70 GOING, Allen J. "The South and the Blair Education Bill." *Miss Val Hist Rev,* XLIV (1957), 267–290.

71 GOLDMAN, Eric F. *Rendezvous with Destiny: A History of Modern American Reform.* New York, 1952.†

72 HAYS, Samuel P. *The Response to Industrialism, 1885-1914*. Chicago, 1957.

73 HIRSHON, Stanley P. *Farewell to the Bloody Shirt: Northern Republicans and the Southern Negro, 1877-1890*. Bloomington, 1962.

74 HOUSE, Albert V. "Republicans and Democrats Search for New Identities, 1870-1890." *Rev Pol*, XXXI (1969), 466-476.

75 JENSEN, Richard Joseph. "The Winning of the Midwest: A Social History of Midwestern Elections, 1888-1896." Doctoral dissertation, Yale University, 1967.

76 JOSEPHSON, Matthew. *The Politicos 1865-1896*. New York, 1938.†

77 KLEPPNER, Paul John. *The Cross of Culture: A Social Analysis of Midwestern Politics, 1850-1900*. New York, 1970.

78 KLEPPNER, Paul John. "The Politics of Change in the Midwest: The 1890's in Historical and Behavorial Perspective." Doctoral dissertation, University of Pittsburgh, 1967.

79 LYDENBURG, John. "Pre-Mucking: A Study of Attitudes toward Politics as Revealed in American Fiction from 1870 through 1901." Doctoral dissertation, Harvard University, 1946.

80 MAYER, George H. *The Republican Party, 1854-1964*. New York, 1964.†

81 MOOS, Malcolm. *The Republicans*. New York, 1956.

82 MORGAN, H. Wayne. *From Hayes to McKinley: National Party Politics*. Syracuse, 1969.

83 MORGAN, H. Wayne, ed. *The Gilded Age: A Reappraisal*. Syracuse, 1963. Rev. ed., 1970.†

84 OBERHOLTZER, Ellis Paxson. *A History of the United States since the Civil War*. 5 vols. New York, 1917-1937.

85 OSTROGORSKI, Moisei. *Democracy and the Organization of Political Parties*. 2 vols. New York, 1902.

86 PECK, Harry Thurston. *Twenty Years of the Republic, 1885-1905*. New York, 1906.

87 RHODES, James Ford. *History of the United States from Hayes to McKinley: 1877-1896*. New York, 1919.

88 ROSEBLOOM, Eugene H. *A History of Presidential Elections*. New York, 1957.

89 SHANNON, Fred A. *The Centennial Years: A Political and Economic History of America from the Late 1870's to the Early 1890's*. Garden City, N.Y., 1967.†

90 STEIN, Charles W. *Third-Term Tradition, Its Rise and Collapse in American Politics*. New York, 1943.

91 WHITE, Leonard D. *The Republican Era 1869-1901: A Study in Administrative History*. New York, 1958.

92 WIEBE, Robert H. *The Search for Order, 1877-1920*. New York, 1967.†

93 WILSON, Woodrow. *Congressional Government: A Study in American Politics*. Boston, 1885.

2. Biographies

94 ABSHIRE, David M. *The South Rejects a Prophet: The Life of Senator D. M. Key, 1824-1900*. New York, 1967.

95 BARNARD, Harry. *Eagle Forgotten, the Life of John Peter Altgeld*. Indianapolis, 1938.

96 BARNARD, Harry. *Rutherford B. Hayes and His America*. Indianapolis, 1954.

97 BARNES, James A. *John G. Carlisle, Financial Statesman*. New York, 1931.

98 BARROWS, Chester L. *William E. Evarts, Lawyer, Diplomat, Statesman*. Chapel Hill, 1941.

99 BASS, Herbert J. *'I Am a Democrat': The Political Career of David Bennett Hill*. Syracuse, 1961.

100 BEER, Thomas. *Hanna*. New York, 1929.

101 BIGELOW, John. *The Life of Samuel J. Tilden*. 2 vols. New York, 1895.

102 BLAKE, Nelson M. *William Mahone of Virginia, Soldier and Political Insurgent*. Richmond, Va., 1935.

103 BROWNE, Waldo R. *Altgeld of Illinois*. New York, 1924.

104 BURTON, Theodore E. *John Sherman*. Boston, 1908.

105 BUSBEY, L. White. *Uncle Joe Cannon*. New York, 1927.

106 BYARS, William V. *An American Commoner: The Life and Times of Richard Parks Bland*. Columbia, Mo., 1900.

107 CALDWELL, Robert G. *James A. Garfield: Party Chieftain*. New York, 1931.

108 CARY, Edward. *George William Curtis*. Boston, 1894.

109 CATE, Wirt Armistead. *Lucius Q. C. Lamar, Secession and Reunion 1825-1893*. Chapel Hill, 1935.

110 CHIDSEY, Donald B. *The Gentleman from New York: A Life of Roscoe Conkling*. New Haven, 1935.

111 CLAPP, Margaret. *Forgotten First Citizen: John Bigelow*. Boston, 1947.

112 COLEMAN, McAlister. *Eugene V. Debs: A Man Unafraid*. New York, 1930.

113 COLETTA, Paolo E. *William Jennings Bryan, I. Political Evangelist, 1860-1908*. Lincoln, Neb., 1964.

114 CONKLING, Alfred R. *The Life and Letters of Roscoe Conkling*. New York, 1889.

115 COOK, J. W. "The Life and Labors of Hon. Adlai Ewing Stevenson." *J Ill State Hist Soc*, VIII (1915), 209-231.

116 CORTISSOZ, Royal. *The Life of Whitelaw Reid*. 2 vols. New York, 1921.

117 COTNER, Robert. *James Stephen Hogg, a Biography.* Austin, 1959.

118 CRAMER, Clarence H. *Royal Bob, The Life of Robert G. Ingersoll.* Indianapolis, 1952.

119 CROLY, Herbert. *Marcus Alonzo Hanna: His Life and Work.* New York, 1912.

120 CRUNDEN, Robert M. *A Hero in Spite of Himself: Brand Whitlock in Art, Politics and War.* New York, 1969.

121 CURRENT, Richard N. *Pine Logs and Politics: A Life of Philetus Sawyer, 1816-1900.* Madison, 1950.

122 DE SANTIS, Vincent P. "Grover Cleveland." *American's Ten Greatest Presidents.* Ed. Morton Borden. Chicago, 1961.

123 DESTLER, Chester M. *Henry Demarest Lloyd and the Empire of Reform.* Philadelphia, 1963.

124 DINGLEY, Edward Nelson. *The Life and Times of Nelson Dingley, Jr.* Kalamazoo, Mich., 1902.

125 DYER, Brainerd. *The Public Career of William M. Evarts.* Berkeley, 1933.

126 ECKENRODE, Hamilton J. *Rutherford B. Hayes, Statesman of Reunion.* New York, 1930.

127 ELLIS, Elmer. *Henry Moore Teller: Defender of the West.* Caldwell, Idaho, 1941.

128 FLICK, Alexander C. *Samuel Jones Tilden: A Study in Political Sagacity.* New York, 1939.

129 FOWLER, Dorothy Ganfield. *John Coit Spooner: Defender of Presidents.* New York, 1961.

130 FUESS, Claude M. *Carl Schurz, Reformer.* New York, 1932.

131 GAMBRELL, H. "James Stephen Hogg: Statesman or Demagogue?" *SW Rev,* XIII (1928), 338-366.

132 GARRATY, John A. *Henry Cabot Lodge, a Biography.* New York, 1953.

133 GEIGER, Louis G. *Joseph W. Folk of Missouri.* Columbia, Mo., 1953.

134 GEORGE, Henry, Jr. *The Life of Henry George.* New York, 1900.

135 GILLETT, Frederick Huntington. *George Frisbie Hoar.* Boston, 1934.

136 GINGER, Ray. *The Bending Cross: Eugene V. Debs.* New Brunswick, 1949.†

137 GLAD, Paul W. *The Trumpet Soundeth: William Jennings Bryan and His Democracy, 1896-1912.* Lincoln, Neb., 1960.†

138 GOODRICH, F. E. *Life of W. S. Hancock.* New York, 1886.

139 GOSNELL, Harold. *Boss Platt and His New York Machine.* Chicago, 1924.

140 GRANTHAM, Dewey W., Jr. *Hoke Smith and the Politics of the New South, 1855-1931.* Baton Rouge, 1958.†

141 GRESHAM, Matilda. *Life of Walter Quintin Gresham.* 2 vols. Chicago, 1919.

142 GWINN, William R. *Uncle Joe Cannon, Archfoe of Insurgency.* New York, 1957.

143 HALSTEAD, Murat. *The Illustrious Life of William McKinley, Our Martyred President.* Chicago, 1901.

144 HAMILTON, Gail, and Mary Abigail DODGE. *Biography of James G. Blaine.* Norwich, Conn., 1895.

145 HAYNES, Frederick E. *James Baird Weaver.* Iowa City, 1919.

146 HIBBEN, Paxton. *The Peerless Leader: William Jennings Bryan.* New York, 1929.

147 HICKS, John D. "The Political Career of Ignatius Donnelly." *Miss Val Hist Rev,* VIII (1921), 80–132.

148 HILL, Benjamin, Jr. *Senator Benjamin H. Hill of Georgia, His Life, Speeches, and Writings.* Atlanta, 1891.

149 HIRSCH, Mark D. *William C. Whitney: Modern Warwick.* New York, 1948.

150 HOLLI, Melvin G. *Reform in Detroit: Hazen S. Pingree and Urban Politics.* New York, 1969.

151 HOLMES, William F. *The White Chief: James Kimble Vardaman.* Baton Rouge, 1970.

152 HOUSE, Albert V. "The Political Career of Samuel Jackson Randall." Doctoral dissertation, University of Wisconsin, 1934.

153 HOWE, George F. *Chester A. Arthur: A Quarter-Century of Machine Politics.* New York, 1934.

154 JAMES, Henry. *Richard Olney and His Public Service.* Boston, 1923.

155 JOHNSON, Carolyn W. *Winthrop Murray Crane: A Study in Republican Leadership, 1892-1920.* Northampton, Mass., 1967.

156 KAPLAN, Justin. *Mr. Clemens and Mark Twain.* New York, 1956.†

157 KATZ, Irving. *August Belmont: A Political Biography.* New York, 1968.

158 KELLER, Morton. *The Art and Politics of Thomas Nast.* New York, 1968.

159 KERR, Winfield S. *John Sherman: His Life and Public Service.* 2 vols. Boston, 1908.

160 LA FOLLETTE, Belle Case, and Fola LA FOLLETTE. *Robert M. La Follette.* 2 vols. New York, 1953.

161 LAMBERT, John R. *Arthur Pue Gorman.* Baton Rouge, 1953.

162 LAMBERT, Oscar D. *Stephen Benton Elkins.* Pittsburgh, 1955.

163 LARSEN, William. *Montague of Virginia: The Making of a Southern Progressive.* Baton Rouge, 1965.

164 LEECH, Margaret. *In the Days of McKinley.* New York, 1959.

165 LEWIS, Alfred Henry. *Richard Croker.* New York, 1901.

166 LINDSEY, David. *"Sunset" Cox Irrepressible Democrat.* Detroit, 1959.

167 LLOYD, Caro. *Henry Demarest Lloyd.* 2 vols. New York, 1912.

168 LONG, John Cuthbert. *Bryan, the Great Commoner.* New York, 1928.

169 LYNCH, Denis T. *Grover Cleveland, the Man and the Statesman.* New York, 1923.

170 MC CALL, Samuel W. *The Life of Thomas B. Reed.* Boston, 1914.

171 MC ELROY, Robert M. *Grover Cleveland, the Man and the Statesman.* 2 vols. New York, 1923.

172 MC ELROY, Robert M. *Levi Parsons Morton: Banker, Diplomat and Statesman.* New York, 1930.

173 MC GURRIN, James. *Bourke Cochran: A Free Lance in American Politics.* New York, 1948.

174 MAGIE, David. *Life of Garret Augustus Hobart.* New York, 1910.

175 MARCOSSON, Isaac F. *"Marse Henry," A Biography of Henry Watterson.* New York, 1951.

176 MAYES, Edward. *Lucius Q. C. Lamar: His Life, Times and Speeches.* Nashville, 1896.

177 MAXWELL, Robert S. *La Follette and the Rise of Progressives in Wisconsin.* Madison, 1956.†

178 MERRILL, Horace Samuel. *Bourbon Leader: Grover Cleveland and the Democratic Party.* Boston, 1957.†

179 MERRILL, Horace Samuel. *William Freeman Vilas: Doctrinaire Democrat.* Madison, 1954.

180 MILNE, Gordon. *George William Curtis and the Genteel Tradition.* Bloomington, 1956.

181 MORGAN, H. Wayne. *William McKinley and His America.* Syracuse, 1963.

182 MUZZEY, David S. *James G. Blaine, a Political Idol of Other Days.* New York, 1934.

183 NASH, Howard, Jr. *Stormy Petrel: The Life and Times of Gen. Benjamin F. Butler, 1818-1893.* Rutherford, N.J., 1969.

184 NEVINS, Allan. *Abram S. Hewitt: With Some Account of Peter Cooper.* New York, 1935.

185 NEVINS, Allan. *Grover Cleveland: A Study in Courage.* New York, 1932.

186 NICHOLS, Jeannette P. "John Sherman: A Study in Inflation." *Miss Val Hist Rev,* XXI (1938), 181-194.

187 NIELSON, James W. *Shelby M. Cullom: Prairie State Republican.* Urbana, Ill., 1962.

188 NOBLIN, Stuart. *Leonidas Lafayette Polk, Agrarian Crusader.* Chapel Hill, 1945.

189 OGDEN, Rollo, ed. *Life and Letters of Edwin Lawrence Godkin.* 2 vols. New York, 1907.

190 OLCOTT, Charles S. *The Life of William McKinley.* 2 vols. Boston, 1916.

191 OLIVER, John W. "Matthew Stanley Quay." *W Pa Hist Mag,* XVII (1934), 1-12.

192 OLSON, James C. *J. Sterling Morton.* Lincoln, Neb., 1942.

193 PAINE, Albert B. *Thomas Nast: His Period and His Pictures.* New York, 1904.

194 PALMER, George T. A. *A Conscientious Turncoat: The Story of John M. Palmer.* New Haven, 1941.

195 PEPPER, Charles M. *The Life and Times of Henry Gassaway Davis, 1823-1916.* New York, 1920.

196 RAWLEY, James A. *Edwin D. Morgan, 1811-1883: Merchant in Politics.* New York, 1955.

197 RICHARDSON, Leon Burr. *William E. Chandler, Republican.* New York, 1940.

198 RIDGE, Martin. *Ignatius Donnelly: The Portrait of a Politician.* Chicago, 1962.

199 RIORDAN, William L. *Plunkitt of Tammany Hall.* New York, 1948.†

200 ROBINSON, William A. *Thomas B. Reed, Parliamentarian.* New York, 1930.

201 RUSSELL, Charles E. *Blaine of Maine: His Life and Times.* New York, 1931.

202 SAGE, Leland L. *William Boyd Allison: A Study in Practical Politics.* Iowa City, 1956.

203 SHAW, Albert. "William V. Allen: Populist." *Rev Rev,* X (1894), 30-42.

204 SIEVERS, Harry J. *Benjamin Harrison: Hoosier President: The White House and After.* New York, 1968.

205 SIEVERS, Harry J. *Benjamin Harrison, Hoosier Statesman: 1865-1888.* New York, 1959.

206 SIMKINS, Francis B. *Pitchfork Ben Tillman, South Carolinian.* Baton Rouge, 1944.†

207 SMITH, Theodore Clarke. *The Life and Letters of James Abram Garfield.* 2 vols. New Haven, 1925.

208 SNYDER, Carl. "Marion Butler." *Rev Rev,* XIV (1896), 427-435.

209 SPIELMAN, William Carl. *William McKinley: Stalwart Republican.* New York, 1954.

210 STANWOOD, Edward. *James Gillespie Blaine.* Boston, 1905.

211 STEPHENSON, Nathaniel Wright. *Nelson W. Aldrich: A Leader in American Politics.* New York, 1930.

212 STODDARD, Lothrop. *Master of Manhattan: The Life of Richard Croker.* New York, 1931.

213 SUMMERS, Festus P. *William L. Wilson and Tariff Reform.* New Brunswick, 1953.

214 TAGER, Jack. *The Intellectual as Urban Reformer: Brand Whitlock and the Progressive Movement.* Cleveland, 1968.

215 TANSILL, Charles C. *The Congressional Career of Thomas Francis Bayard, 1868-1885.* Washington, D.C., 1946.

216 TARR, Joel A. "William Lorimer of Illinois: A Study in Boss Politics." Doctoral dissertation, Northwestern University, 1963.

217 TIMMONS, Bascom N. *Portrait of an American: Charles G. Davis.* New York, 1953.

218 TUGWELL, Rexford G. *Grover Cleveland.* New York, 1968.

219 WALL, Joseph Frazier. *Henry Watterson: Reconstructed Rebel.* New York, 1956.

220 WALTERS, Everett. *Joseph Benson Foraker: An Uncompromising Republican.* Columbus, Ohio, 1948.

221 WEBB, Ross A. *Benjamin Helm Bristow: Border State Politician.* Lexington, Ky., 1969.

222 WEISS, Nancy Joan. *Charles Francis Murphy, 1858-1924: Respectability and Responsibility in Tammany Politics.* Northampton, Mass., 1968.

223 WELCH, Richard E., Jr. "George Edmunds of Vermont: Republican Half-breed." *Vt Hist,* XXXVI (1968), 64-73.

224 WERNER, Morris Robert. *Bryan.* New York, 1929.

225 WEST, Richard S., Jr. *Lincoln's Scapegoat General: A Life of Benjamin F. Butler, 1818-1893.* Boston, 1965.

226 WHITE, William Allen. *Masks in a Pageant.* New York, 1928.

227 WILLIAMS, Charles R. *The Life of Rutherford B. Hayes.* 2 vols. Boston, 1914.

228 WOODWARD, C. Vann. *Tom Watson: Agrarian Rebel.* New York, 1938.†

229 YOUNGER, Edward. *John A. Kasson: Politics and Diplomacy from Lincoln to McKinley.* Iowa City, 1955.

3. Autobiographies, Memoirs, Reminiscences, Diaries, Printed Letters and Speeches, and Collected Works

230 ADAMS, Henry. *The Education of Henry Adams.* Boston, 1918.†

231 BARRY, David S. *Forty Years in Washington.* Boston, 1924.

232 BEALE, H. S. B., ed. *Letters of Mrs. James G. Blaine.* New York, 1908.

233 BELMONT, Perry. *American Democrat: The Recollections of Perry Belmont.* 2d ed. New York, 1967.

234 BIGELOW, John. *Retrospections of an Active Life.* 5 vols. New York, 1909.

235 BLAINE, James G. *Political Discussions.* Norwich, Conn., 1887.

236 BLAINE, James G. *Twenty Years in Congress.* 2 vols. Norwich, Conn., 1884-1886.

237 BOUTWELL, George S. *Reminiscences of Sixty Years in Public Affairs.* New York, 1902.

238 BROWN, George R., ed. *Reminiscences of William M. Stewart of Nevada.* New York, 1908.

239 BROWN, Harry J., and F. D. WILLIAMS, eds. *The Diary of James A. Garfield.* East Lansing, Mich., 1967- .

240 BRYAN, Mary B., ed. *The Memoirs of William Jennings Bryan.* Philadelphia, 1925.

241 BRYAN, William J. *The First Battle.* Chicago, 1896.

242 BRYAN, William J. *Speeches of William Jennings Bryan.* 2 vols. New York, 1913.

243 BUTLER, Joseph G., Jr. *Presidents I Have Seen and Known.* Cleveland, 1910.

244 BUTLER, Joseph G., Jr. *Recollection of Men and Events.* Youngstown, Ohio, 1925.

245 CARPENTER, Francis, ed. *Carp's Washington.* New York, 1960.

246 COX, Samuel Sullivan. *Three Decades of Federal Legislation, 1855-1885.* Washington, D.C., 1885.

247 CULLOM, Shelby M. *Fifty Years of Public Service.* Chicago, 1911.

248 DAWES, Charles G. *A Journal of the McKinley Years, 1893-1913.* Chicago, 1950.

249 DEPEW, Chauncey M. *My Memories of Eighty Years.* New York, 1922.

250 DOW, Neal. *The Reminiscences of Neal Dow.* Portland, Me., 1898.

251 DUNN, Arthur W. *From Harrison to Harding: A Personal Narrative Covering a Third of a Century, 1888-1921.* 2 vols. New York, 1922.

252 FORAKER, Joseph B. *Notes of a Busy Life.* Cincinnati, 1916.

253 FORAKER, Julia B. *I Would Live It Again.* New York, 1932.

254 FORD, Worthington C., ed. *The Letters of Henry Adams, 1858-1891.* Boston, 1930.

255 FORNEY, John W. *Anecdotes of Public Men.* 2 vols. New York, 1873-1881.

256 FOSTER, John W. *Diplomatic Memoirs.* 2 vols. Boston, 1909.

257 FOULKE, William Dudley. *Fighting the Spoilsmen; Reminiscences of the Civil Service Reform Movement.* New York, 1919.

258 GLADDEN, Washington. *Recollections.* Boston, 1909.

259 GODKIN, Edwin L. *Reflections and Comments 1865-1895.* New York, 1896.

260 GRANT, Ulysses S. *Personal Memoirs.* 2 vols. New York, 1885-1886.†

261 GRINNELL, Josiah B. *Men and Events of Forty Years.* Boston, 1891.

262 HANCOCK, Almira Russell, ed. *Reminiscences of Winfield Scott Hancock.* New York, 1887.

263 HARRISON, Benjamin. *This Country of Ours.* New York, 1901.

264 HARRISON, Mary Lord, comp. *Views of an Ex-President.* Indianapolis, 1901.

265 HEDGES, Charles, ed. *Speeches of Benjamin Harrison.* New York, 1892.

266 HILLQUIT, Morris. *Loose Leaves from a Busy Life.* New York, 1934.

267 HINSDALE, Burke A., ed. *The Works of James A. Garfield.* 2 vols. Boston, 1882.

268 HINSDALE, Mary L., ed. *Garfield-Hinsdale Letters: Correspondence between James Abram Garfield and Burke Aaron Hinsdale.* Ann Arbor, 1949.

269 HOAR, George Frisbie. *Autobiography of Seventy Years.* 2 vols. New York, 1903.

270 HUDSON, W. C. *Random Recollections of an Old Political Reporter.* New York, 1911.

271 JOHNSON, Robert U. *Remembered Yesterdays.* Boston, 1923.

272 JOHNSON, Tom L. *My Story.* New York, 1911.

273 KOHLSATT, H. H. *From McKinley to Harding.* New York, 1923.

274 LA FOLLETTE, Robert M. *La Follette's Autobiography.* Madison, 1918.

275 LINK, Arthur S., et al., eds. *The Papers of Woodrow Wilson.* Vols. I-IX. Princeton, 1966-1970.

276 LODGE, Henry Cabot, ed. *Selections from the Correspondence of Theodore Roosevelt and Henry Cabot Lodge.* 2 vols. New York, 1925.

277 LYNCH, John R. *Reminiscences of an Active Life: The Autobiography.* Chicago, 1970.

278 MC CLURE, S. S. *My Autobiography.* New York, 1914.

279 MC CULLOCH, Hugh. *Men and Measures of a Half Century.* New York, 1888.

280 NEVINS, Allan, ed. *The Letters and Journals of Brand Whitlock.* 2 vols. New York, 1936.

281 NEVINS, Allan, ed. *Letters of Grover Cleveland, 1850-1908.* Boston, 1933.

282 NORTON, Charles Eliot, ed. *Orations and Addresses of George William Curtis.* New York, 1894.

283 PALMER, John M. *Personal Recollections: The Story of an Earnest Life.* Cincinnati, 1901.

284 PARKER, George F. *Recollections of Grover Cleveland.* New York, 1909.

285 PARKER, George F., ed. *Writings and Speeches of Grover Cleveland.* New York, 1892.

286 PENDEL, Thomas F. *Thirty-Six Years in the White House.* Washington, D.C., 1902.

287 PLATT, Thomas Collier. *The Autobiography of Thomas Collier Platt.* New York, 1910.

288 POORE, Benjamin. *Perley's Reminiscences of Sixty Years in the National Metropolis.* 2 vols. Philadelphia, 1886.

289 ROOSEVELT, Theodore. *Autobiography.* New York, 1912.

290 ROSSITER, Will. *McKinley Memoirs.* Chicago, 1901.

291 SCHURZ, Carl. *Reminiscences.* 3 vols. New York, 1907-1908.

292 SCHURZ, Carl. *Speeches, Correspondence, and Political Papers.* Ed. Frederic Bancroft. 6 vols. New York, 1913.

293 SEWARD, Frederick W. *Reminiscences of a Wartime Statesman and Diplomat, 1830-1915.* New York, 1916.

294 SHERMAN, John. *John Sherman's Recollections of Forty Years in House, Senate and Cabinet.* 2 vols. Chicago and New York, 1895.

295 *Speeches and Addresses of William McKinley.* New York, 1900.

296 STEALEY, Orlando O. *Twenty Years in the Press Gallery.* New York, 1906.

297 STEVENSON, Adlai E. *Something of Men I Have Known.* Chicago, 1909.

298 STEWART, William M. *Reminiscences.* New York, 1908.

299 STODDARD, Henry Luther. *As I Knew Them: Presidents and Politics from Grant to Coolidge.* New York, 1927.

300 STRAUS, Oscar S. *Under Four Administrations: From Cleveland to Taft.* New York, 1922.

301 SUMMERS, Festus P., ed. *The Cabinet Diary of William L. Wilson, 1896-1897.* Chapel Hill, 1957.

302 THORNDIKE, Rachel Sherman. *The Sherman Letters.* New York, 1894.

303 TILDEN, Samuel J. *Letters.* New York, 1908.

304 TILDEN, Samuel J. *The Writings and Speeches of Samuel J. Tilden.* New York, 1885.

305 VARE, William S. *My Forty Years in Politics.* Philadelphia, 1933.

306 VILLARD, Henry. *Memoirs.* 2 vols. Boston, 1904.

307 VOLWILER, Albert T., ed. *The Correspondence between Benjamin Harrison and James G. Blaine.* Philadelphia, 1940.

308 WATTERSON, Henry. *"Marse Henry," an Autobiography.* 2 vols. New York, 1919.

309 WHEELER, Everett P. *Sixty Years of American Life.* New York, 1917.

310 WHITE, Andrew D. *Autobiography of Andrew Dickson White.* 2 vols. New York, 1905.

311 WHITE, William Allen. *The Autobiography of William Allen White.* New York, 1946.

312 WILLIAMS, Charles R., ed. *The Diary and Letters of Rutherford Birchard Hayes.* 5 vols. Columbus, Ohio, 1922-1926.

313 WILLIAMS, T. Harry., ed. *Hayes: The Diary of a President 1875-1881.* New York, 1964.

314 WISE, John S. *Recollections of Thirteen Presidents.* New York, 1906.

4. From Hayes to Cleveland, 1877-1897

315 ADAMS, Charles Francis, Jr. "What Mr. Cleveland Stands For." *Forum*, XIII (1892), 662-672.

316 BABCOCK, Joseph W. "The Meaning of the Election." *N Amer Rev*, CLIX (1894), 742-754.

317 BARKER, Wharton. "The Secret History of Garfield's Nomination." *Pear Mag*, XXXV (1916), 435-443.

318 BARNARD, Harry. *Rutherford B. Hayes.* See 96.

319 BARROWS, Chester L. *William E. Evarts.* See 98.

320 BEER, Thomas. *The Mauve Decade: American Life at the End of the Nineteenth Century.* New York, 1926.

321 BERNARDO, C. J. "The Presidential Election of 1888." Doctoral dissertation, Georgetown University, 1949.

322 BLODGETT, Geoffrey. *The Gentle Reformers: Massachusetts Democracy in the Cleveland Era.* Cambridge, Mass., 1966.

323 BROWN, Harry J., and F. D. WILLIAMS. *Diary of Garfield.* See 239.

324 BROWN, Wenzell. "Hayes, the Forgotten President." *Am Mercury*, LXVIII (1949), 169-177.

325 BRUCE, R. V. *1877: Year of Violence.* Indianapolis, 1959.†

326 BULEY, R. C. "Campaign of 1888 in Indiana." *Ind Mag Hist*, X (1914), 30-53.

327 BURGESS, John W. *The Administration of President Hayes.* New York, 1916.

328 CALDWELL, Robert G. *James A. Garfield.* See 107.

329 CHIDSEY, Donald. *Roscoe Conkling.* See 110.

330 CLANCY, Herbert J. *The Presidential Election of 1880.* Chicago, 1958.

331 CLEVELAND, Grover. *Presidential Problems.* New York, 1904.

332 COLETTA, Paolo E. "Bryan, Cleveland, and the Disrupted Democracy, 1890-1896." *Neb Hist*, XLIV (1963), 167-187.

333 CONNERY, T. B. "Secret History of the Garfield-Conkling Tragedy." *Cosmopolitan*, XXIII (1897), 145-162.

334 COOK, J. W. "The Life and Labors of Hon. Adlai E. Stevenson." See 115.

335 DAWES, Henry L. "Garfield and Conkling." *Century*, XLVII (1893-1894), 341-344.

336 DE SANTIS, Vincent P. "Benjamin Harrison and the Republican Party in the South, 1889-1893." *Ind Mag Hist*, LI (1955), 279-302.

337 DE SANTIS, Vincent P. "President Arthur and the Independent Movements in the South, in 1882." *J S Hist*, XIX (1953), 346-363.

338 DE SANTIS, Vincent P. "President Garfield and the Solid South." *NC Hist Rev*, XXXVI (1959), 442-465.

339 DE SANTIS, Vincent P. "President Hayes' Southern Policy." *J S Hist*, XXI (1955), 476-494.

340 DOBSON, John M. "George William Curtis and the Election of 1884: The Dilemma of the New York Mugwumps." *NY Hist Soc Q*, LII (1968), 215-234.

341 DOZER, Donald M. "Benjamin Harrison and the Presidential Campaign of 1892." *Am Hist Rev*, LIV (1948), 49-77.

342 DYER, Brainerd. *Public Career of William M. Evarts*. See 125.

343 ECKENRODE, Hamilton J. *Rutherford B. Hayes*. See 126.

344 EWING, J. S. "Mr. Stevenson, the Democratic Candidate for Vice President." *Rev Rev*, XXII (1900), 420-424.

345 FLICK, Alexander C. *Samuel Jones Tilden*. See 128.

346 FORD, Henry Jones. *The Cleveland Era*. New Haven, 1921.

347 FUESS, Claude M. *Carl Schurz*. See 130.

348 FUESS, Claude M. "Schurz, Lodge and the Campaign of 1884." *N Eng Q*, V (1932), 453-482.

349 GARRISON, Curtis W. "Conversation with Hayes: A Biographer's Notes." *Miss Val Hist Rev*, XXV (1938), 368-380.

350 GINGER, Ray. *Altgeld's America*. New York, 1958.†

351 GLADDEN, Washington. "The Embattled Farmers." *Forum*, X (1890), 315-322.

352 GOODRICH, F. E. *W. S. Hancock*. See 138.

353 HARRISON, Mary Lord, comp. *Views of an Ex-President*. See 264.

354 HAWORTH, Paul L. *The Hayes-Tilden Disputed Presidential Election of 1876*. Cleveland, 1906.

355 HAYES, Rutherford B. *Letters and Messages, Together with Letter of Acceptance and Inaugural Address*. Washington, D.C., 1881.

356 HAYNES, Frederick E. *James Baird Weaver*. See 144.

357 HEDGES, Charles, ed. *Speeches of Harrison*. See 265.

358 HICKS, John. *The Populist Revolt*. Minneapolis, 1931.†

359 HIRSCH, Mark D. "Samuel J. Tilden: The Story of a Lost Opportunity." *Am Hist Rev*, LVI (1951), 788-802.

360 HIRSCH, Mark D. *William C. Whitney*. See 148.

361 HOFFMAN, Charles. "The Depression of the Nineties." *J Econ Hist*, XVI (1956), 137-164.

362 HOLLINGSWORTH, J. Rogers. *The Whirligig of Politics: The Democracy of Cleveland and Bryan*. Chicago, 1963.

363 HOUSE, Albert V. "Internal Conflicts in Key States in the Democratic Convention of 1880." *Pa Hist*, XXVII (1960), 188-216.

364 HOUSE, Albert V. "President Hayes' Selection of David M. Key for Postmaster General." *J S Hist*, IV (1938). 87-93.

365 HOWE, George F. *Chester A. Arthur.* See 152.

366 HOWE, George F. "President Hayes' Notes of Four Cabinet Meetings." *Am Hist Rev*, XXXVII (1931), 286-289.

367 JAMES, Henry. *Richard Olney.* See 154.

368 KERR, Winfield Scott. *John Sherman.* See 159.

369 KLOTSCHE, J. Martin. "Star Route Cases." *Miss Val Hist Rev*, XXII (1935), 407-418.

370 KNOLES, George H. "Populism and Socialism with Special Reference to the Election of 1892." *Pac Hist Rev*, XII (1943), 295-304.

371 KNOLES, George H. *The Presidential Campaign and Election of 1892.* Palo Alto, Calif., 1942.

372 KREBS, Frank John. "Hayes and the South." Doctoral dissertation, Ohio State University, 1950.

373 LAUCK, William Jett. *The Causes of the Panic of 1893.* New York, 1907.

374 LINDSEY, Almont. *The Pullman Strike.* Chicago, 1942.†

375 LYNCH, Denis T. *Grover Cleveland: The Man and the Statesman.* See 169.

376 LYNCH, Denis T. *The Wild Seventies.* New York, 1941.

377 MC ELROY, Robert M. *Grover Cleveland.* See 171.

378 MC FARLAND, Gerald W. "The Breakdown of Deadlock: The Cleveland Democracy in Connecticut, 1884-1894." *Hist*, XXXI (1969), 381-397.

379 MC GRANE, Reginald Charles. "Ohio and the Greenback Movement." *Miss Val Hist Rev*, XI (1924-1925), 526-542.

380 MACK, Frank W. "Rum, Romanism and Rebellion." *Har Week*, XLVIII (1904), 1140-1142.

381 MC MURRY, Donald L. *Coxey's Army.* Boston, 1929.†

382 MC MURRY, Donald L. "Pension Bureau during Harrison." *Miss Val Hist Rev*, XIII (1926), 343-364.

383 MC MURRY, Donald L. "Pension Question." *Miss Val Hist Rev*, IX (1922), 19-36.

384 MC PHERSON, James M. "Coercion or Conciliation? Abolitionists Debate President Hayes's Southern Policy." *New Eng Q*, XXXIX (1966), 474-497.

385 MALIN, James C. "Roosevelt and Elections of 1884 and 1888." *Miss Val Hist Rev*, XIV (1927), 25-38.

386 MERRILL, Horace Samuel. *Grover Cleveland.* See 179.

387 MITCHELL, Stewart. "The Man Who Murdered Garfield." *Proc Mass Hist Soc*, LXVII (1944), 452-489.

388 NEVINS, Allan. *Grover Cleveland.* See 185.

389 NEVINS, Allan, ed. *Letters of Grover Cleveland, 1850-1908.* See 181.

390 NEWCOMER, Lee. "Arthur's Removal from the Customs House." *NY Hist*, XVIII (1938), 401-410.

391 NICHOLS, Jeannette P. "The Politics and Personalities of Silver Repeal in the United States Senate." *Am Hist Rev* (1935), 26-53.

392 NICHOLS, Jeannette P. "Rutherford B. Hayes and John Sherman." *Ohio Hist Q*, LXXVII (1968), 125-138.

393 NICHOLS, Jeannette P. "Sherman and the Silver Drive of 1877-78." *Ohio State Arch Hist Q*, XLVI (1937), 148-165.

394 OLSON, James C. *J. Sterling Morton.* See 192.

395 PARKER, George F. *Recollections of Cleveland.* See 284.

396 PARKER, George F., ed. *Writings and Speeches of Cleveland.* See 285.

397 PAYNE, Thomas. "The Administration Theory and Practice of Grover Cleveland." Doctoral dissertation, University of Chicago, 1951.

398 PESKIN, Allan. "Garfield and Hayes, Political Leaders of the Gilded Age." *Ohio Hist Q*, LXXVII (1968), 111-124.

399 PLETCHER, David M. *The Awkward Years: Foreign Policy under Garfield and Arthur.* Columbia, Mo., 1962.

400 RAE, John B. "Commissioner Sparks and Railroad Land Grants." *Miss Val Hist Rev*, XXV (1938), 211-230.

401 RANDOLPH, Carmen. "Surplus Revenue." *Pol Sci Q*, III (1888), 226-246.

402 REEVES, Thomas C. "Chester A. Arthur and Campaign Assessments in the Election of 1880." *Hist*, XXXI (1969), 573-583.

403 REEVES, Thomas C. "Chester A. Arthur and the Campaign of 1880." *Pol Sci Q*, LXXXIV (1969), 628-637.

404 REZNECK, Samuel. "Distress, Relief, and Discontent during Depression of 1873-1878." *J Pol Econ*, LVIII (1950), 494-512.

405 REZNECK, Samuel. "Unemployment, Unrest, Relief in the United States during the Depression of 1893-1897." *J Pol Econ*, LXI (1953), 324-345.

406 RICHARDSON, Lyon N., and Curtis W. GARRISON. "Curtis, Hayes, and Civil Service Reform." *Miss Val Hist Rev*, XXXII (1945), 235-250.

407 ROSENBERG, Charles E. *The Trial of the Assassin Guiteau: Psychiatry and Law in the Gilded Age.* Chicago, 1968.

408 SEITZ, Don C. *The Dreadful Decade.* Indianapolis, 1926.

409 SHERMAN, John. *Recollections.* See 284.

410 SHORES, Venila L. *The Hayes-Conkling Controversy.* New York, 1919.

411 SIEVERS, Harry J. *Benjamin Harrison.* See 204.

412 SINKLER, George. "Benjamin Harrison and the Matter of Race." *Ind Mag Hist*, LXV (1969), 197-215.

413 SINKLER, George. "Race: Principles and Policies of Rutherford B. Hayes." *Ohio Hist Q*, LXXVII (1968), 149-167.

414 SMALLEY, E. V. "Characteristics of President Garfield." *Cent Illus Month Mag*, XXIII (1881-1882), 168-176.

415 SMITH, Theodore Clarke. *Life and Letters of James A. Garfield.* See 207.

416 STEAD, W. T. "Coxeyism: A Character Sketch." *Am Rev Rev*, X (1894), 47-59.

417 STROBEL, Edward H. *Mr. Blaine and His Foreign Policy.* Boston, 1884.

418 SUMMERS, Festus P. *William L. Wilson and Tariff Reform.* See 213.

419 SUMMERS, Festus P., ed. *The Cabinet Diary of William L. Wilson.* See 301.

420 TAUSSIG, Frank W. *The Silver Situation in the United States.* New York, 1892.

421 TAUSSIG, Frank W. "The United States Treasury, 1894-1896." *Q J Econ*, XIII (1899), 204-218.

422 THELEN, David P. "Rutherford B. Hayes and the Reform Tradition in the Gilded Age." *Am Q*, XXII (1970), 150-165.

423 THOMAS, Harrison C. *The Return of the Democratic Party to Power in 1884.* New York, 1919.

424 TUGWELL, Rexford G. *Grover Cleveland.* See 218.

425 TUNNELL, George. "Legislative History of the Second Income Tax." *J Pol Econ*, III (1895), 311-337.

426 TYLER, Alice Felt. *The Foreign Policy of James G. Blaine.* Minneapolis, 1927.

427 VAN DEUSEN, John G. "Did Republicans 'Colonize' Indiana in 1879?" *Ind Mag Hist*, XXX (1935), 335-346.

428 VINCENT, Henry. *The Story of the Commonweal.* Chicago, 1894.

429 VOLWILER, Albert T., ed. "Tariff Strategy and Propaganda, 1887-88." *Am Hist Rev*, XXXVI (1930), 76-96.

430 WEAVER, James B. *A Call to Action.* Des Moines, Iowa, 1892.

431 WEBERG, F. B. *The Background of the Panic of 1893.* Washington, D.C., 1929.

432 WELCH, Richard E., Jr. "The Federal Election Bill of 1890: Postscripts and Prelude." *J Am Hist*, LII (1965), 511-526.

433 WELLBORN, Fred. "The Influence of the Silver-Republican Senators, 1889-1891." *Miss Val Hist Rev*, XIV (1928), 462-472.

434 WELLS, O. V. "Depression of 1873-79." *Ag Hist*, XI (1937), 237-249.

435 WHITE, Edward Arthur. "The Republican Party in National Politics, 1888-1891." Doctoral dissertation, University of Wisconsin, 1941.

436 WILLIAMS, Charles R., ed. *Diary and Letters of Hayes.* See 312.

437 WILLIAMS, Charles R. *The Life of Hayes.* See 227.

438 WILLIAMS, T. Harry., ed. *Diary of a President.* See 313.

439 WOLFF, Leon. *Lockout: The Story of the Homestead Strike of 1892.* New York, 1965.

440 WOODWARD, C. Vann. *Reunion and Reaction: The Compromise of 1877 and the End of Reconstruction.* Boston, 1951.†

IV. American Politics from the Agrarian Crusade to William McKinley

441 ABBEY, Kathryn T. "Florida versus the Principles of Populism." *J S Hist,* IV (1938), 462-475.

442 ABRAMOWITZ, Jack. "The Negro in the Agrarian Revolt." *Ag Hist,* XXIV (1950), 89-95.

443 ABRAMOWITZ, Jack. "The Negro in the Populist Movement." *J Neg Hist,* XXXVIII (1953), 257-289.

444 ABRAMS, Richard M., ed. *The Issues of the Populist and Progressive Eras, 1892-1912.* Columbia, S.C., 1969.

445 ADAMS, Charles Francis, Jr. "The Granger Movement." *N Am Rev,* CXX (1875), 394-424.

446 ADAMS, Herbert B., ed. *History of Cooperation in the United States.* Baltimore, 1888.

447 ALDRICH, Charles R. "Repeal of the Granger Law in Iowa." *Iowa J Hist Pol,* III (1905), 256-270.

448 ALLEN, W. H. "The Election of 1900." *Ann Am Acad,* XVII (1901), 54-73.

449 ALLEN, William V. "Western Feeling Towards the East." *N Am Rev,* CLXII (1896), 588-593.

450 ANDER, O. Fritiof. "The Immigrant Church and the Patrons of Husbandry." *Ag Hist,* VIII (1934), 155-168.

451 ANDERSON, William A. "The Granger Movement in the Middle West with Special References to Iowa." *Iowa J Hist Pol,* XXII (1924), 3-51.

452 ARGERSINGER, Peter H. "Road to a Republican Waterloo: The Farmers Alliance and the Election of 1900 in Kansas." *Kan Hist Q,* XXXIII (1967), 443-469.

453 ARNETT, Alex M. *The Populist Movement in Georgia.* New York, 1922.

454 ASHBY, N. B. *The Riddle of the Sphinx.* Des Moines, Iowa, 1890.

455 BAILEY, Thomas A. "Was the Presidential Election of 1900 a Mandate on Imperialism?" *Miss Val Hist Rev,* XXIV (1937-1938), 43-52.

456 BARNES, James A. "The Gold Standard Democrats and Party Conflict." *Miss Val Hist Rev*, XVII (1930), 422-450.

457 BARNES, James A. "Illinois and the Gold-Silver Controversy, 1890-1896." *Tran Ill State Hist Soc* (1931), 35-39. Springfield, Ill., 1932.

458 BARNES, James A. "Myths of the Bryan Campaign." *Miss Val Hist Rev*, XXXIV (1947), 367-404.

459 BARNHART, John D. "Rainfall and the Populist Party in Nebraska." *Am Pol Sci Rev*, XIX (1925), 522-540.

460 BARNS, William. "The Granger and Populist Movements in West Virginia, 1873-1914." Doctoral dissertation, West Virginia University, 1947.

461 BARNS, William D. "Oliver H. Kelley and the Genesis of the Grange: A Reappraisal." *Ag Hist*, XLI (1967), 229-242.

462 BARTON, R. H. "The Agrarian Revolt in Michigan, 1865-1900." Doctoral dissertation, Michigan State Univesity, 1958.

463 BEALS, Carleton. *The Great Revolt and Its Leaders: The History of Popular American Uprisings in the 1890's*. New York, 1968.

464 BEARD, Earl S. "The Background of State Railroad Regulation in Iowa." *Iowa J Hist*, LI (1953), 1-36.

465 BEER, Thomas. *Hanna*. See 100.

466 BERSTEIN, Irving, ed. "Samuel Gompers and Free Silver." *Miss Val Hist Rev*, XXIX (1942), 394-400.

467 BICHA, Karel Denis. "A Further Reconsideration of American Populism." *Mid-Am*, LII (1971), 3-11.

468 BICHA, Karel Denis. "Jerry Simpson: Populist without Principle." *J Am Hist*, LIV (1967), 291-306.

469 BLOOD, F. G. *Handbook and History of the National Farmer's Alliance and Industrial Union*. Washington, D.C., 1893.

470 BRODHEAD, Michael. *Persevering Populist: The Life of Frank Doster*. Reno, Nev., 1969.

471 BROOKS, Robert P. *The Agrarian Revolution in Georgia, 1865-1912*. Madison, 1914.

472 BROWNE, Waldo Ralph. *Altgeld of Illinois*. See 103.

473 BRUDVIG, Glenn Lowell. "The Farmers' Movement and the Populist Movement in North Dakota (1884-1896)." M. A. thesis, University of North Dakota, 1956.

474 BRYAN, J. E. *The Farmers' Alliance: Its Origin, Progress and Purposes*. Fayette, Ark., 1891.

475 BRYAN, Mary B., ed. *The Memoirs of William Jennings Bryan*. See 240.

476 BRYAN, William J. *The First Battle*. See 241.

477 BRYAN, William J. *The Second Battle*. Chicago, 1900.

478 BRYAN, William J. *Speeches of William Jennings Bryan*. See 242.

479 BUCK, Solon J. *The Agrarian Crusade*. New Haven, 1920.

480 BUCK, Solon J. "Agricultural Organization in Illinois, 1870-1880." *J Ill State Hist Soc*, III (1910-1912), 10-23.

481 BUCK, Solon J. *The Granger Movement.* Cambridge, Mass., 1913. †

482 BUTLER, Joseph G., Jr. *Presidents I Have Seen and Known.* See 243.

483 BUTLER, Joseph G., Jr. *Recollection of Men and Events.* See 244.

484 BUTLER, Marion. "The People's Party." *Forum*, XXVIII (1900), 658-662.

485 CANFIELD, James, et al. "A Bundle of Western Letters." *Rev Rev*, X (1894), 42-46.

486 CHAFE, William H. "The Negro and Populism: A Kansas Case Study." *J S Hist*, XXXIV (1968), 402-419.

487 CHAPPLE, Joe Mitchell. *Mark Hanna: His Book.* Boston, 1904.

488 CLANTON, O. Gene. "Intolerant Populist? The Disaffection of Mary Elizabeth Lease." *Kan Hist Q*, XXXIV (1968), 189-200.

489 CLANTON, O. Gene. *Kansas Populism: Ideas and Men.* Lawrence, Kan., 1969.

490 CLARK, John B. *Populism in Alabama.* Auburn, Ala., 1927.

491 CLEVENGER, Homer. "Agrarian Politics in Missouri, 1880-1896." Doctoral dissertation, University of Missouri, 1940.

492 CLINCH, Thomas A. *Urban Populism and Free Silver in Montana: A Narrative Ideology in Political Action.* Missoula, Mont., 1970.

493 COLETTA, Paolo E. *William Jennings Bryan.* See 113.

494 COLWELL, J. L. "Populist Image of Vernon L. Parrington." *Miss Val Hist Rev*, XLIX (1962), 52-56.

495 CONRAD, Frederick Allen. "Agrarian Movements in the United States since the Civil War: A Study in Class Conflict." Doctoral dissertation, Stanford University, 1933.

496 CORNWALL, William G. *Free Coinage from the Businessman's Standpoint.* Buffalo, N.Y., 1891.

497 CRAWFORD, Harriet P. "Grange Attitudes in Washington, 1889-1896." *Pac N W Q*, XXX (1939), 243-274.

498 CROLY, Herbert. *Marcus Alonzo Hanna.* See 119.

499 CROWE, Charles. "Tom Watson, Populists, and Blacks Reconsidered." *J Neg Hist*, LV (1970), 99-116.

500 DANIEL, Lucia E. "The Louisiana People's Party." *La Hist Q*, XXVI (1943), 1055-1149.

501 DAVIS, Granville D. "The Granger Movement in Arkansas." *Ark Hist Q*, IV (1945), 340-352.

502 DAWES, Charles G. *A Journal of the McKinley Years.* See 248.

503 DESTLER, Chester M. "Agricultural Readjustment and Agrarian Unrest in Illinois, 1880-1896." *Ag Hist*, XXI (1947), 104-116.

504 DESTLER, Chester M. "Consummation of a Labor-Populist Alliance in Illinois, 1894." *Miss Val Hist Rev*, XXVII (1941), 589-602.

505 DETRICK, Charles R. "The Effects of the Granger Acts." *J Pol Econ*, XI (1903), 237-256.

506 DIAMOND, William. "Urban and Rural Voting in 1896." *Am Hist Rev*, XLVI (1941), 281-305.

507 DIGGS, Annie L. "The Farmers Alliance and Some of Its Leaders." *Arena*, V (1892), 590-604.

508 DINGLEY, Edward Nelson. *The Life and Times of Nelson Dingley, Jr.* See 124.

509 DONNELLY, Ignatius. *The American People's Money*. Chicago, 1895.

510 DOSTER, James F. "Were Populists against Railroad Corporations? The Case of Alabama." *J S Hist*, XX (1954), 395-399.

511 DREW, Frank. "The Present Farmer's Movement." *Pol Sci Q*, V (1891), 282-310.

512 DURDEN, Robert F. *The Climax of Populism: The Election of 1896.* Lexington, Ky., 1965.†

513 DURDEN, Robert F. "The 'Cow-Bird' Grounded: The Populist Nomination of Bryan and Watson in 1896." *Miss Val Hist Rev*, L (1963), 397-423.

514 EASTERBY, J. H. "The Granger Movement in South Carolina." *S C Hist Assn Proc*, I (1931), 21-32.

515 EDSALL, James K. "The Granger Cases and the Police Power." *Rep Am Bar Assn*, X (1887), 288-316.

516 ELLIS, Elmer. *Henry Moore Teller: Defender of the West.* See 127.

517 ELLIS, Elmer. "The Silver Republicans in the Election of 1896." *Miss Val Hist Rev*, XVIII (1932), 519-543.

518 EMERICK, C. F. "An Analysis of Agricultural Discontent in the United States." *Pol Sci Q*, XI (1896), 433-463, 601-639; XII (1897), 93-127.

519 FAIRCHILD, G. T. "Populism in a State Education Institution, the Kansas State Agricultural College." *Am J Socio*, III (1897), 392-404.

520 FARMER, Hallie. "The Economic Background of Frontier Populism." *Miss Val Hist Rev*, X (1924), 406-427.

521 FARMER, Hallie. "The Economic Background of Southern Populism." *S Atl Q*, XXIX (1930), 77-91.

522 FARMER, Hallie. "The Railroads and Frontier Populism." *Miss Val Hist Rev*, XIII (1926), 389-397.

523 FERGUSON, James S. "Agrarianism in Mississippi, 1871-1900, a Study in Nonconformity." Doctoral dissertation, University of North Carolina, 1952.

524 FERGUSON, James S. "Grange and Farmer Education in Mississippi." *J S Hist*, VIII (1942), 497-512.

525 FERKISS, Victor C. "Populism: Myth, Reality, Current Danger." *W Pol Q*, XIV (1961), 737-780.

526 FERKISS, Victor C. "The Populist Influence on American Fascism." *W Pol Q*, X (1957), 350-373.

527 FINE, Nathan. *Labor and Farmer Parties in the United States 1828-1928.* New York, 1928.

528 FINNERAN, Helen T. "Records of the National Grange in Its Washington Office." *Am Archiv*, XXVII (1964), 103-111.

529 FISHER, Willard. "'Coin' and His Critics." *Q J Econ*, X (1896), 187-208.

530 FITE, Gilbert C. "Republican Strategy and the Farm Vote in the Presidential Campaign of 1896." *Am Hist Rev*, XLV (1960), 787-806.

531 FITE, Gilbert. C. "William Jennings Bryan and the Campaign of 1896: Some Views and Problems." *Neb Hist*, XLVII (1966), 247-264.

532 FLOWER, Edward. "Anti-Semitism in the Free Silver and Populist Movement and the Election of 1896." M. A. thesis, Columbia University, 1952.

533 FLYNN, J. T. "Mark Hanna." *Scrib Mag*, XCIV (1933), 85-90.

534 FONDA, Arthur I. *Honest Money.* New York, 1895.

535 FORAKER, Julia B. *I Would Live It Again.* See 253.

536 FOSSUM, Paul R. *The Agrarian Movement in North Dakota.* Baltimore, 1925.

537 FOSTER, Florence J. "The Grange and Cooperative Enterprises in New England." *Ann Am Acad Pol Soc Sci*, IV (1894), 798-805.

538 FULLER, Leon W. "Colorado's Revolt against Capitalism." *Miss Val Hist Rev*, XXI (1934), 343-360.

539 FULLER, Wayne E. "The Grange in Colorado." *Colo Mag*, XXXVI (1959), 254-265.

540 GALAMBOS, Louis. "The Agrarian Image of the Large Corporation, 1869-1920: A Study in Social Accomodation." *J Econ Hist*, XXVIII (1968), 341-362.

541 GARLAND, Hamlin. "The Alliance Wedge in Congress." *Arena*, V (1892), 447-457.

542 GLAD, Paul W. *McKinley, Bryan and the People.* Philadelphia, 1964.†

543 GLASS, Mary Ellen. *Silver and Politics in Nevada: 1892-1902.* Reno, Nev., 1969.

544 GLAZER, Sidney. "Labor and the Agrarian Movements in Michigan, 1876-1896." Doctoral dissertation, University of Michigan, 1932.

545 GNATZ, William R. "The Negro and the Populist Movement in the South." M.A. thesis, University of Chicago, 1961.

546 GRIFFITHS, David. "Far West Populism: The Case of Utah 1892-1900." *Utah Hist Q*, XXXVII (1969), 396-407.

547 HACKNEY, Sheldon. *Populism to Progressivism in Alabama.* Princeton, 1969.

548 HAIR, William Ivy. *Bourbonism and Agrarian Protest: Louisiana Politics, 1877-1900.* Baton Rouge, 1969.

549 HALL, Tom G. "California Populism at the Grass Roots: The Case of Tulare County, 1892." *S Calif Q*, XLIX (1967), 193-204.

550 HALSTEAD, Murat. *The Illustrious Life of William McKinley, Our Martyred President.* Chicago, 1901. See 143.

551 HANDLIN, Oscar. "Reconsidering the Populist." *Ag Hist*, XXXIX (1965), 68-74.

552 HARGER, Charles M. "New Era in the Middle West." *Har Mag*, XCVII (1898), 276-282.

553 HART, Roger. "Bourbonism and Agrarianism in Tennessee." Doctoral dissertation, Princeton University, 1970.

554 HARVEY, William Hope. *Coin's Financial School.* Chicago, 1894.†

555 HAYNES, Frederick E. *James Baird Weaver.* See 144.

556 HAYNES, Frederick E. "The New Sectionalism." *Q J Econ*, X (1896), 269-295.

557 HAYNES, Frederick E. *Third Party Movements since the Civil War.* Iowa City, 1916.

558 HIBBEN, Paxton. *The Peerless Leader; William Jennings Bryan.* See 145.

559 HICKS, John D. "The Birth of the Populist Party." *Minn Hist*, IX (1928), 219-248.

560 HICKS, John D. "The Farmers' Alliance in North Carolina." *N Car Hist Rev*, XI (1925), 162-187.

561 HICKS, John D. "The Legacy of Populism in the Western Middle West." *Ag Hist*, XXIII (1949), 225-236.

562 HICKS, John D. "The Origin and Early History of the Farmers' Alliance in Minnesota." *Miss Val Hist Rev*, IX (1922), 203-226.

563 HICKS, John D. "Our Pioneer Heritage: A Reconsideration." *Prairie Schooner*, XXX (1956), 359-361.

564 HICKS, John D. "The People's Party in Minnesota." *Minn Hist Bull*, V (1924), 531-560.

565 HICKS, John D. "The Political Career of Ignatius Donnelly." See 146.

566 HICKS, John D. *The Populist Revolt.* See 358.†

567 HICKS, John D. "Some Parallels with Populism in the Twentieth Century." *Soc Ed*, VIII (1944), 297-301.

568 HICKS, John D. "The Sub-Treasury: A Forgotten Plan for the Relief of Agriculture." *Miss Val Hist Rev*, XV (1928), 355-373.

569 HIRSCH, Arthur H. "Efforts of the Grange in Middle West to Control Price of Farm Machinery 1870-1880." *Miss Val Hist Rev*, XV (1929), 473-496.

570 HOFFMAN, Charles. "The Depression of the Nineties." See 361.

571 HOFSTADTER, Richard. *The Age of Reform: From Bryan to FDR.* New York, 1955.†

572 HOLBO, Paul S. "Wheat or What? Populism and American Fascism." *W Pol Q*, XIV (1961), 727-736.

573 HOLLINGSWORTH, J. Rogers. "Populism: The Problem of Rhetoric and Reality." *Ag Hist*, XXXIX (1965), 81-85.

574 HOLLINGSWORTH, J. Rogers. *The Whirligig of Politics*. See 362.

575 HUNT, Robert Lee. *A History of Farmer Movements in the Southwest, 1873-1925*. College Station, Tex., 1935.

576 INGLE, H. Larry. "A Southern Democrat at Large: William Hodge Kitchin and the Populist Party." *N C History Rev*, XLV (1968), 178-195.

577 JONES, Stanley L. *The Presidential Election of 1896*. Madison, 1964.

578 KASSON, John A. "Impressions of President McKinley." *Cent Mag*, LXI (1901), 269-275.

579 KELLEY, Oliver Hudson. *Origin and Progress of the Order of Patrons of Husbandry*. Philadelphia, 1875.

580 KENDRICK, Benjamin J. "Agrarian Discontent in the South, 1880-1900." *Ann Rep Am Hist Assoc*, 1920. Washington, D.C., 1925, pp. 265-272.

581 KENNEDY, Roger G. "Ignatius Donnelly and the Politics of Discontent." *Am West*, VI (1969), 10-14, 43, 46-48.

582 KIRWAN, Albert D. *The Revolt of the Rednecks: Mississippi Politics, 1876-1925*. Lexington, Ky., 1951.†

583 KLOTSCHE, Martin J. "The 'United Front' Populists." *Wis Mag Hist*, XI (1937), 275-389.

584 KNAUSS, James O. "The Farmers' Alliance in Florida." *S Atl Q*, XXV (1926), 300-315.

585 KNOLES, George H. "Populism and Socialism with Special Reference to the Election of 1892." See 370.

586 KNOLES, George H. *The Presidential Campaign and Election of 1892*. See 371.

587 KOHLSATT, H. H. *From McKinley to Harding*. See 273.

588 KOLKO, Gabriel. *Railroads and Regulation, 1877-1916*. Princeton, 1965.†

589 LAUGHLIN, J. Laurence. "Causes of Agricultural Unrest." *Atl Month*, LXXVIII (1896), 577-585.

590 LAUGHLIN, J. Laurence. *Facts About Money*. Chicago, 1895.

591 LEECH, Margaret. *In the Days of McKinley*. See 164.

592 LIBBY, Orin G. "A Study of the Greenback Movement." *Tran Wis Acad*, LXXII (1898), 530-545.

593 LLOYD, Henry Demarest. "The Populists at St. Louis." *Rev Rev*, XIV (1896), 293-303.

594 LODGE, Henry Cabot. "The Meaning of the Votes [1896 election]." *N Am Rev*, CLXV (1897), 1-11.

595 LONG, John Cuthbert. *Bryan, the Great Commoner*. See 168.

596 LONG, John D. "Some Personal Characteristics of President McKinley." *Cent Mag*, XLIII (1901), 144-146.

597 MC VEY, Frank Le Rond. "The Populist Movement." *Selected Readings in Rural Economics.* T. N. Carver, comp. Boston, 1916.

598 MC VEY, Frank Le Rond. *The Populist Movement.* New York, 1896.

599 MAGIE, David. *Life of Garret Augustus Hobart.* See 174.

600 MALIN, James C. "The Farmers' Alliance Subtreasury Plan and European Precedents." *Miss Val Hist Rev,* XXXI (1944), 255-260.

601 MALIN, James C. "Notes on the Literature of Populism." *Kan Hist Q,* I (1932), 160-164.

602 MANNING, Joseph C. *The Fadeout of Populism.* New York, 1928.

603 MARTIN, Roscoe C. *The People's Party in Texas.* Austin, 1933.†

604 MERK, Frederick. "Eastern Antecedents of the Grangers." *Ag Hist,* XXIII (1949), 1-8.

605 MILLER, George H. "Origin of the Iowa Granger Law." *Miss Val Hist Rev,* XL (1954), 657-680.

606 MILLER, Raymond C. "The Background of Populism in Kansas." *Miss Val Hist Rev,* XI (1925), 469-489.

607 MILLER, Raymond C. "The Populist Party in Kansas." Doctoral dissertation, University of Chicago, 1928.

608 MOGER, Allen W. "The Rift in the Virginia Democracy in 1896." *J S Hist,* IV (1938), 295-317.

609 MORGAN, H. Wayne. *William McKinley and His America.* See 181.

610 MORGAN, T. W. Scott. *History of the Wheel and Alliance.* Fort Scott, Kan., 1889.

611 NICHOLS, Jeannette P. "Bryan's Benefactor: Coin Harvey and His World." *Ohio Hist Q,* LXVII (1958), 299-325.

612 NIXON, Herman C. "The Cleavage within the Farmers' Alliance Movement." *Miss Val Hist Rev,* XV (1928), 22-33.

613 NIXON, Herman C. "The Economic Basis of the Populist Movement in Iowa." *Iowa J Hist Pol,* XXI (1923), 373-396.

614 NIXON, Herman C. "The Populist Movement in Iowa." *Iowa J Hist Pol,* XXIV (1926), 3-107.

615 NOBLIN, Stuart. *Leonidas La Fayette Polk, Agrarian Crusader.* See 188.

616 NORDIN, Dennis S. "A Revisionist Interpretation of the Patrons of Husbandry, 1867-1900." *Hist,* XXXII (1970), 630-643.

617 NUGENT, Walter T. K. "Some Parameters of Populism." *Ag Hist,* XL (1966), 255-270.

618 NUGENT, Walter T. K. *The Tolerant Populists, Kansas, Populism and Nativism.* Chicago, 1963.

619 NYDEGGER, Walter E. "The Election of 1892 in Iowa." *Iowa J Hist Pol,* XXV (1927), 359-449.

620 NYE, Russel B. *Midwestern Progressive Politics: A Historical Study of Its Origins and Development, 1870-1958.* East Lansing, Mich., 1959.

621 OLCOTT, Charles S. *The Life of William McKinley.* See 190.

622 PAINE, Arthur E. *The Granger Movement in Illinois.* Urbana, Ill., 1904.

623 PALMER, George T. A. *The Story of John M. Palmer.* See 194.

624 PALMER, John M. *Personal Recollections.* See 283.

625 PARSONS, Stanley B. "Who Were the Nebraska Populists?" *Neb Hist,* XLIV (1963), 83–99.

626 PAUL, Rodman W. "The Great California Grain War: The Grangers Challenge the Wheat King." *Pac Hist Rev,* XXVII (1958), 331–349.

627 PEFFER, William A. "The Farmers' Defensive Movement." *Forum,* XVIII (1889), 464–473.

628 PEFFER, William A. *The Farmer's Side, His Troubles and Their Remedy.* New York, 1891.

629 PEFFER, William A. "The Mission of the Populist Party." *N Amer Rev,* CLVII (1893), 665–678.

630 PEFFER, William A. "The Passing of the People's Party." *N Amer Rev,* CLXVI (1898), 12–23.

631 POLLACK, Norman. "Fear of Men: Populism, Authoritarianism, and the Historian." *Ag Hist,* XXXIX (1965), 59–67.

632 POLLACK, Norman. "Hofstadter on Populism: A Critique of 'The Age of Reform.'" *J S Hist,* XXVI (1960), 478–500.

633 POLLACK, Norman. "The Myth of Populist Anti-Semitism." *Am Hist Rev,* LXVIII (1962), 76–80.

634 POLLACK, Norman. *The Populist Mind.* Indianapolis, 1967.†

635 POLLACK, Norman. *The Populist Response to Industrial America: Midwestern Populist Thought.* Cambridge, Mass., 1962.†

636 REZNECK, Samuel. "Unemployment, Unrest, Relief in the United States during the Depression of 1893–1897." See 405.

637 RICE, Stuart A. *Farmers and Workers in American Politics.* New York, 1924.

638 RIDGE, Martin. "Ignatius Donnelly and the Granger Movement in Minnesota." *Miss Val Hist Rev,* XLII (1956), 693–709.

639 RIDGE, Martin. *Ignatius Donnelly: Portrait of a Politician.* See 198.

640 ROBISON, Daniel M. *Bob Taylor and the Agrarian Revolt in Tennessee.* Chapel Hill, 1935.

641 ROBISON, Daniel M. "Tennessee Politics and the Agrarian Revolt, 1886–1896." *Miss Val Hist Rev,* XX (1933), 365–380.

642 ROCHESTER, Anna. *The Populist Movement in the United States.* New York, 1943.

643 ROGERS, William Warren. *The One-Gallused Rebellion: Agrarianism in Alabama, 1865–1896.* Baton Rouge, 1970.

644 ROGIN, Michael. "California Populism and the 'System of 1896.'" *W Pol Q,* XXII (1969), 179–196.

645 ROSSITER, Will. *McKinley Memoirs.* See 290.

646 ROZWENC, Edwin C. "The Group Basis of Vermont Farm Politics, 1870-1945." *Vt Hist,* XXV (1957), 268-287.

647 RUSS, W. A., Jr. "Godkin Looks at Western Agrarianism: A Case Study." *Ag Hist,* XIX (1945), 233-242.

648 SALOUTOS, Theodore. *Farmer Movements in the South, 1865-1933.* Berkeley and Los Angeles, 1960.†

649 SALOUTOS, Theodore. "The Grange and the South, 1870-1877." *J S Hist,* XIX (1953), 473-487.

650 SALOUTOS, Theodore. "The Professors and the Populists." *Ag Hist,* XL (1966), 235-254.

651 SAUNDERS, Robert. "Southern Populists and the Negro, 1893-1905." *J Neg Hist,* LIV (1969), 240-262.

652 SCHELL, Herbert S. "The Granges and the Credit Problem in Dakota." *Ag Hist,* X (1936), 59-83.

653 SCHMIDT, Louis B. "The Role and Techniques of Agrarian Pressure Groups." *Ag Hist,* XXX (1956), 49-58.

654 SCHMIDT, Louis B. "Some Significant Aspects of the Agrarian Revolution in the United States." *Iowa J Hist Pol,* XXVIII (1920), 371-395.

655 SCOTT, Roy V. *The Agrarian Movement in Illinois, 1880-1897.* New York, 1945.†

656 SHANNON, Fred A. *American Farmers' Movements.* Princeton, 1957.†

657 SHANNON, Fred A. "C. W. Macune and the Farmers' Alliance." *Cur Hist,* XXVIII (1955), 330-335.

658 SHANNON, Fred A. *The Farmers' Last Frontier: Agriculture, 1860-1897.* New York, 1945.†

659 SHAW, Albert. "William V. Allen: Populist." See 203.

660 SHELDON, William Du Bose. *Populism in the Old Dominion.* Princeton, 1935.

661 SHILS, Edward. "Populism and the Rule of Law." The Law School of the University of Chicago, Conference on Jurisprudence and Politics, April 30, 1957, pp. 91-107.

662 SIMKINS, Francis B. "Ben Tillman's View of the Negro." *J S Hist,* III (1937), 161-174.

663 SIMKINS, Francis B. *Pitchfork Ben Tillman, South Carolinian.* See 206.†

664 SIMKINS, Francis B. *The Tillman Movement in South Carolina.* Durham, N.C., 1926.

665 SMALLEY, Eugene. "William McKinley—A Study of His Character and Career." *Am Rev Rev,* XIV (1896), 33-45.

666 SMITH, J. Harold. "History of the Grange in Kansas, 1883-1897." M. A. thesis, University of Kansas, 1940.

667 SMITH, Ralph A. "The Cooperative Movement in Texas, 1870-1900." *S W Hist Q*, XLIV (1940), 33-54.

668 SMITH, Ralph A. "The Farmers' Alliance in Texas, 1875-1900." *S W Hist Q*, XLVIII (1945), 346-369.

669 SMITH, Ralph A. "The Grange Movement in Texas, 1873-1900." *S W Hist Q*, XLII (1939), 297-315.

670 SMITH, Ralph A. "'Macuneism,' or the Farmers of Texas in Business." *J S Hist*, XIII (1947), 220-244.

671 SMITH, Robert W. "Comedy at St. Louis: A Footnote to Nineteenth Century Political Oratory." *Speech J*, XXV (1959), 122-133.

672 SNYDER, Carl. "Marion Butler." See 208.

673 *Speeches and Addresses of William McKinley.* See 295.

674 SPIELMAN, William Carl. *William McKinley: Stalwart Republican.* See 209.

675 SPRATT, John S. *The Road to Spindletop: Economic Change in Texas, 1875-1901.* Dallas, 1955.

676 STEWART, Ernest D. "The Populist Party in Indiana." *Ind Mag Hist*, XIV (1918), 332-367; XV (1919), 53-74.

677 TAGGART, Harold F. "California and the Silver Question in 1895." *Pac Hist Rev*, VI (1937), 249-269.

678 TARBELL, Ida. "President McKinley in War Time." *McClure's Mag*, II (1898), 209-224.

679 TAYLOR, Carl C. *The Farmers' Movements, 1620-1920.* New York, 1953.

680 THRONE, Mildred. "The Grange in Iowa, 1868-1875." *Iowa J Hist*, XLVII (1949), 289-324.

681 THRONE, Mildred. "The Repeal of the Iowa Granger Law, 1878." *Iowa J Hist*, LI (1953), 97-103.

682 TINDALL, George B. *A Populist Reader.* New York, 1966.†

683 TRACY, Frank Basil. "The Rise and the Doom of the Populist Party." *Forum*, XVI (1893), 241-250.

684 TRYON, Warren S. "Agriculture and Politics in South Dakota, 1889-1900." *S D Hist Coll*, XIII (1926), 284-310.

685 TUCKER, William P. "Ezra Pound, Fascism and Populism." *J Pol*, XVIII (1956), 105-107.

686 UNGER, Irwin. "Critique of Norman Pollack's 'Fear of Man.'" *Ag Hist*, XXXIX (1965), 75-80.

687 VEBLEN, Thorstein B. "Price of Wheat since 1867." *J Pol Econ*, I (1892), 68-103.

688 WALKER, Francis A. "The Free Coinage of Silver." *J Pol Econ*, I (1893), 163-178.

689 WALKER, Kenneth. "The Third Assassination [McKinley; 1901]." *NY Hist Soc Q*, XLI (1957), 407-422.

690 WARNER, Donald F. "The Farmers' Alliance and the Farmers' Union. An American-Canadian Parallelism." *Ag Hist*, XXIII (1949), 9-19.

691 WARNER, Donald F. "Prelude to Populism." *Minn Hist*, XXII (1949), 129-146.

692 WATSON, Thomas E. "The People's Party Appeal." *Independent*, LVII (1904), 829.

693 WATSON, Thomas E. "Why I Am Still a Populist." *Rev Rev*, XXXVIII (1908), 303-306.

694 WEAVER, James B. *A Call to Action*. Des Moines, Iowa, 1892.

695 WERNER, M. R. *Bryan*. See 224.

696 WEST, Henry Littlefield. "The President's [McKinley's] Recent Tour." *Forum*, XXXI (1900), 661-669.

697 WEST, Henry Littlefield. "William McKinley." *Forum*, XXXII (1901), 131-137.

698 WESTIN, Alan. "The Supreme Court, the Populist Movement, and the Campaign of 1896." *J Pol*, XV (1953), 3-41.

699 WHITE, Melvin J. "Populism in Louisiana during the Nineties." *Miss Val Hist Rev*, V (1918), 3-19.

700 WHITE, William Allen. *Autobiography*. See 311.

701 WHITE, William Allen. "The End of an Epoch." *Scrib Mag*, LXX (1926), 561-570.

702 WHITE, William Allen. *Masks in a Pageant*. See 226.

703 WHITEHEAD, Mortimer. "The Grange in Politics." *Am J Pol*, I (1892), 113-123.

704 WILCOX Benton H. "An Historical Definition of Northwestern Radicalism." *Miss Val Hist Rev*, XXVI (1939), 377-394.

705 WILCOX, Benton H. "A Reconsideration of the Character and Economic Basis of Northwestern Radicalism." Doctoral dissertation, University of Wisconsin, 1933.

706 WILHOIT, Francis M. "An Interpretation of Populism's Impact on the Georgia Negro." *J Neg Hist*, LII (1967), 116-127.

707 WISH, Harvey. "John P. Altgeld and the Background of the Campaign of 1896." *Miss Val Hist Rev*, XXIV (1938), 503-518.

708 WISH, Harvey. "John Peter Altgeld and the Election of 1896." *J Ill State Hist Soc*, XXX (1937), 353-384.

709 WOODBURN, James A. "Western Radicalism in American Politics." *Miss Val Hist Rev*, XIII (1926), 143-168.

710 WOODWARD, C. Vann. *Origins of the New South, 1877-1913*. Baton Rouge, 1951.†

711 WOODWARD, C. Vann. "The Populist Heritage and the Intellectual." *Am Sch*, LIX (1959-1960), 55-72.

712 WOODWARD, C. Vann. *Tom Watson: Agrarian Rebel*. See 228.†

713 WOODWARD, C. Vann. "Tom Watson and the Negro." *J S Hist*, IV (1938), 14-33.

714 WOODY, Carroll H. "Populism in Washington: A Study of the Legislature in 1897." *Wash Hist Q*, XXI (1930), 103-119.

V. Special Aspects of Politics

715 BAILEY, Thomas A. "Party Irregularity in the Senate of the United States, 1869-1901." *S W Pol Sci Q*, XI (1931), 335-354.

716 BAILEY, Thomas A. "The West and Radical Legislation, 1890." *Am Jour Econ Socio*, XXXVIII (1933), 603-611.

717 BINKLEY, Wilfred E. *The President and Congress.* New York, 1962.†

718 BISHOP, Joseph B. "The Secret Ballot in Thirty-Three States." *Forum*, XII (1892), 589-598.

719 BURKE, Albie. "Federal Regulation of Congressional Elections in Northern Cities, 1871-1894." *Am J Legal Hist*, XIV (1970), 17-34.

720 BURNHAM, W. D. *Presidential Ballots, 1836-1892.* See 44.

721 DANA, Richard Henry. "Sir William Harcourt and the Australian Ballot Law." *Proc Mass Hist Soc*, LVIII (1925), 401-418.

722 DEARING, Mary R. *Veterans in Politics; the Story of the G. A. R.* Baton Rouge, 1952.

723 DESTLER, Chester M. *American Radicalism, 1865-1901: Essays and Documents.* New London, Conn., 1946.†

724 DESTLER, Chester M. "Western Radicalism, 1865-1901: Concepts and Origins." *Miss Val Hist Rev*, XXXI (1941), 335-368.

725 ELLIS, Elmer. "Public Opinion on the Income Tax, 1860-1900." *Miss Val Hist Rev*, XXVII (1940), 225-242.

726 ELY, Richard T. *Recent American Socialism.* Baltimore, 1885.

727 EVANS, Elden Cobb. *A History of the Australian Ballot System in United States.* Chicago, 1917.

728 EWING, Cortez A. M. *Presidential Elections, from A. Lincoln to F. D. Roosevelt.* Norman, Okla., 1940.

729 FINE, Nathan. *Labor and Farmer Parties in the United States.* See 527.

730 FLETCHER, Ralph, and Mildred FLETCHER. "Consistency in Party Voting from 1886-1932." *Soc Forces*, XV (1936), 281-285.

731 FREDMAN, L. E. *The Australian Ballot: The Story of an American Reform.* East Lansing, Mich., 1968.

732 FULLER, Hubert Bruce. *Speakers of the House.* Boston, 1909.

733 GALLOWAY, G. B. *History of the House of Representatives.* New York, 1961.

734 GILMAN, Nicholas Paine. *Socialism and the American Spirit.* Boston and New York, 1893.

735 GLASSON, William Henry. *Federal Military Pensions in the United States.* New York, 1918.

736 GRANTHAM, Dewey W., Jr. *The Democratic South.* Athens, Ga., 1963.†

737 HATCH, Lewis C., and Earl SHOUP. *A History of the Vice Presidency of the United States.* New York, 1943.

738 HAYNES, Frederick E. *Social Politics in the United States.* Boston and New York, 1924.

739 HAYNES, Frederick E. *Third Party Movements since the Civil War.* Iowa City, 1916.

740 HAYNES, G. H. *The Senate of the United States: Its History and Practice.* New York, 1960.

741 HICKS, John D. "Third Party Tradition in American Politics." *Miss Val Hist Rev,* XX (1933), 3-28.

742 HILLQUIT, Morris. *History of Socialism in the United States.* New York, 1903.

743 HYMAN, Sidney. *The American President.* New York, 1954.

744 LAIDLER, Harry W. *Social-Economic Movements: An Historical and Comparative Survey of Socialism, Communism, Cooperation, Utopianism and Other Systems of Reform and Reconstruction.* New York, 1949.†

745 LONN, Ella. "Reconciliation between North and South." *J S Hist,* XIII (1947), 3-26.

746 LORANT, Stephen. *The Presidency.* New York, 1951.

747 MC MURRY, Donald L. "The Political Significance of the Pension Question, 1885-1897." *Miss Val Hist Rev,* IX (1922), 19-36.

748 MC NEILL, Neil. *Forge of Democracy: The House of Representatives.* New York, 1963.

749 MAC RAE, Duncan, Jr., and Charles GILBERT. "Critical Elections in Illinois, 1888-1958." *Am Pol Sci Rev,* LIX (1960), 669-683.

750 MERRILL, Horace Samuel. *Bourbon Democracy of the Middle West, 1865-1898.* Baton Rouge, 1953.†

751 O' GRADY, Joseph P. "The Roman Question in American Politics, 1885." *J Ch State,* X (1968), 365-377.

752 OLIVER, John William. *History of the Civil War Pensions, 1861-1885.* Madison, 1917.

753 QUINT, Howard. *The Forging of American Socialism: Origins of the Modern Movement.* New York, 1953.†

754 RIKER, William. "The Senate and American Federalism." *Am Pol Sci Rev,* XLIX (1955), 452-469.

755 ROACH, Hannah Grace. "Sectionalism in Congress, 1870 to 1890." *Am Pol Sci Rev*, XIX (1925), 500-526.

756 ROTHMAN, David J. *Politics and Power, the United States Senate, 1869-1901.* Cambridge, Mass., 1966.†

757 RUSS, William A., Jr. "Congressional Disfranchisement 1866-1898." Doctoral dissertation, University of Chicago, 1933.

758 SHANNON, David A. *The Socialist Party of America.* New York, 1955.†

759 STANWOOD, Edward. *A History of the Presidency.* 2 vols. Boston, 1921.

760 WHITE, Leonard D. *The Republican Era 1869-1901: A Study in Administrative History.* See 91.†

761 WILSON, Woodrow. *Congressional Government: A Study in American Politics.* See 93.

762 WYNES, Charles E. *Forgotten Voices: Dissenting Southerners in an Age of Conformity.* Baton Rouge, 1967.

VI. State and Local Politics

763 ALLSWANG, John M. *Ethnic Politics in Chicago, 1890-1936.* Lexington, Ky., 1970.

764 BAILEY, Hugh C. *Edgar Gardner Murphy: Gentle Progressive.* Coral Gables, Fla., 1968.

765 BAILEY, Hugh C. *Liberalism in the New South: Southern Social Reformers and the Progressive Movement.* Coral Gables, Fla., 1969.

766 BARNARD, Harry. *The Life of John Peter Altgeld.* See 95.

767 BARNARD, Harry. *Rutherford B. Hayes.* See 96.

768 BASS, Herbert J. *The Political Career of David Bennett Hill.* See 99.

769 BEAN, Walton. *Boss Ruef's San Francisco: The Story of the Union Labor Party, Big Business and the Graft Prosecution.* Berkeley, 1952.†

770 BEER, Thomas. *Hanna.* See 100.

771 BENJAMIN, Philip. "Gentlemen Reformers in the Quaker City, 1870-1912." *Pol Sci Q*, LXXXV (1970), 61-79.

772 BENSON, Lee. *Merchants, Farmers, and Railroads: Railroad Regulation and New York Politics, 1850-1887.* Cambridge, Mass., 1955.

773 BLAKE, Nelson M. *William Mahone of Virginia.* See 102.

774 BLODGETT, Geoffrey. *The Gentle Reformers: Massachusetts Democrats in the Cleveland Era.* See 322.

775 BOUTWELL, George S. *Reminiscences of Sixty Years.* See 237.

776 BREMNER, Robert H. *From the Depths: The Discovery of Poverty in the United States.* New York, 1956.†

777 BROOKS, Aubrey L. *Walter Clark, Fighting Judge.* Chapel Hill, 1944.

778 BROOKS, Aubrey L., and Hugh T. LEFLER, eds. *The Papers of Walter Clark.* 2 vols. Chapel Hill, 1948-1949.

779 CALLOW, Alexander B., Jr. *The Tweed Ring.* New York, 1966.†

780 CASDORPH, Paul. *A History of the Republican Party in Texas, 1865-1965.* Austin, 1965.

781 CHESSMAN, G. Wallace. *Governor Theodore Roosevelt; The Albany Apprenticeship, 1898-1900.* Cambridge, Mass., 1965.

782 CHIDSEY, Donald. *Roscoe Conkling.* See 110.

783 CHURCH, Charles A. *History of the Republican Party in Illinois, 1854-1912.* Rockford, Ill., 1912.

784 CLAPP, Margaret. *John Bigelow.* See 111.

785 CLINCH, Thomas A. *Urban Populism and Free Silver in Montana.* See 492.

786 CONNABLE, Alfred, and Edward SILBERFORB. *Tigers of Tammany: Nine Men Who Ran New York.* New York, 1967.

787 CONNOR, Seymour V. *Texas: A History.* New York, 1971.

788 COOPER, William J., Jr. *The Conservative Regime: South Carolina, 1877-1890.* Baltimore, 1968.

789 COTNER, Robert. *James Stephen Hogg, a Biography.* See 117.

790 CROLY, Herbert. *Marcus Alonzo Hanna.* See 119.

791 CROOKS, James B. *Politics and Progress: The Rise of Urban Progressivism in Baltimore, 1895-1911.* Baton Rouge, 1968.

792 CRUNDEN, Robert M. *A Hero in Spite of Himself: Brand Whitlock in Art, Politics and War.* See 120.

793 CULLOM, Shelby M. *Fifty Years of Public Service.* See 247.

794 CURRENT, Richard N. *A Life of Philetus Sawyer.* See 121.

795 DAVIS, Allen F. "Settlement Workers in Politics, 1890-1941." *Rev Pol,* XXVI (1964), 505-517.

796 DAVIS, Allen F. *Spearhead for Reform: The Social Settlements and the Progressive Movement, 1890-1914.* New York, 1967.†

797 DELMATIER, Royce, Clarence MC INTOSH, and Earl WATERS, eds. *The Rumble of California Politics, 1848-1970.* New York, 1970.†

798 DOBSON, John M. "George William Curtis and the Election of 1884: The Dilemma of the New York Mugwumps." See 340.

799 DOHERTY, Herbert J., Jr. "Voices of Protest from the New South, 1875-1910." *Miss Val Hist Rev,* XLII (1955), 45-66.

800 DOSTER, James F. *Railroads in Alabama Politics, 1875-1914.* University, Ala., 1951.

801 ELLIS, Elmer. *Henry Moore Teller.* See 127.

802 EVANS, Frank B. *Pennsylvania Politics, 1872-1877: A Study in Political Leadership.* Harrisburg, Pa., 1966.

803 FERRELL, Henry C., Jr. "Prohibition, Reform and Politics in Virginia, 1895-1916." *Pub Hist (E Car Col)*, III (1966), 175-242.

804 FINE, Sidney. "Richard T. Ely, Forerunner of Progressivism, 1880-1901." *Miss Val Hist Rev*, XXXVII (1951), 599-624.

805 FLICK, Alexander C. *Samuel Jones Tilden.* See 128.

806 FLINT, Winston A. *The Progressive Movement in Vermont.* Washington, D.C., 1941.

807 FOGELSON, Robert M. *The Fragmented Metropolis: Los Angeles, 1850-1930.* Cambridge, Mass., 1967.

808 FOWLER, Dorothy Ganfield. *John Coit Spooner.* See 129.

809 GAMBRELL, H. "James Stephen Hogg." See 131.

810 GARRATY, John A. *Henry Cabot Lodge.* See 132.

811 GEIGER, Louis G. *Joseph W. Folk of Missouri.* See 133.

812 GIBSON, Elizabeth. *The Attitudes of the New York Irish toward State and National Affairs, 1848-1892.* New York, 1951.

813 GILLETT, Frederick Huntington. *George Frisbie Hoar.* See 135.

814 GLASS, Mary Ellen. *Silver and Politics in Nevada.* See 543.

815 GOING, Allen J. *Bourbon Democracy in Alabama, 1874-1890.* University, Ala., 1951.

816 GOSNELL, Harold. *Boss Platt and His New York Machine.* See 139.

817 GOULD, Lewis L. *Wyoming: A Political History, 1869-1896.* New Haven, 1968.

818 GRANTHAM, Dewey W., Jr. *Hoke Smith and the Politics of the New South.* See 140.†

819 GREEN, Constance. *Washington: Capitol City, 1879-1950.* Princeton, 1953.

820 GRESHAM, Matilda. *Life of Walter Quintin Gresham.* See 141.

821 HACKNEY, Sheldon. *Populism to Progressivism in Alabama.* See 547.

822 HAIR, William Ivy. *Bourbonism and Agrarian Protest: Louisiana Politics, 1877-1900.* See 548.

823 HALSELL, Willie D. "The Bourbon Period in Mississippi Politics, 1875-1890." *J S Hist*, XI (1945), 519-537.

824 HALSELL, Willie D. "James R. Chalmers and Mahoneism in Mississippi." *J S Hist*, X (1944), 37-58.

825 HALSELL, Willie D., ed. "Republican Factionalism in Mississippi, 1882-1884." *J S Hist*, VII (1941), 84-101.

826 HESSELTINE, William B. *Confederate Leaders in the New South.* Baton Rouge, 1950.

827 HILL, Benjamin, Jr. *Senator Benjamin H. Hill.* See 148.

828 HOAR, George Frisbie. *Autobiography*. See 269.

829 HOLLI, Melvin G. *Reform in Detroit: Hazen S. Pingree and Urban Politics.* See 150.

830 HOUSE, Albert V. "The Political Career of Samuel Jackson Randall." See 152.

831 HOWARD, Perry H. *Political Tendencies in Louisiana: 1812-1952*. Baton Rouge, 1957.

832 HOWE, George F. *Chester A. Arthur*. See 153.

833 ISAAC, Paul E. *Prohibition and Politics: Turbulent Decades in Tennessee, 1885-1920*. Knoxville, Tenn., 1965.

834 JACKSON, Joy J. *New Orleans in the Gilded Age: Politics and Urban Progress, 1880-1896*. Baton Rouge, 1969.

835 JOHNSON, Carolyn W. *Winthrop Murray Crane*. See 155.

836 JOHNSON, Tom L. *My Story*. See 272.

837 JORDAN, Philip D. *Ohio Comes of Age, 1870-1900*. Columbus, Ohio, 1943.

838 KERR, Winfield Scott. *John Sherman*. See 159.

839 KIRWAN, Albert D. "Apportionment in the Mississippi Constitution of 1890." *J S Hist*, XIV (1948), 234-246.

840 KIRWAN, Albert D. *The Revolt of the Rednecks*. See 582.†

841 LAMAR, Howard F. *Dakota Territory: 1861-1889: A Study of Frontier Politics*. New Haven, 1956.†

842 LAMAR, Howard F. *The Far Southwest, 1846-1912*. New Haven, 1966.†

843 LAMBERT, John R. *Arthur Pue Gorman*. See 161.

844 LAMBERT, Oscar D. *Stephen Benton Elkins*. See 162.

845 LARSEN, William. *Montague of Virginia: The Making of a Southern Progressive*. See 163.

846 LEWIS, Alfred Henry. *Richard Croker*. See 165.

847 LEWIS, Oscar. *Silver Kings: The Lives and Times of Mackay, Fair, Flood, and O'Brien, Lords of the Nevada Comstock Lode*. New York, 1947.

848 LINK, Arthur S. "The Progressive Movement in the South, 1870-1914." *N Car Hist Rev*, XXIII (1946), 172-195.

849 MC CALL, Samuel W. *The Life of Thomas B. Reed*. See 170.

850 MC CULLOCH, Hugh. *Men and Measures of a Half Century*. See 279.

851 MC ELROY, Robert M. *Grover Cleveland*. See 171.

852 MC ELROY, Robert M. *Levi Parsons Morton*. See 172.

853 MC FARLAND, Gerald W. "The Breakdown of Deadlock: The Cleveland Democracy in Connecticut, 1884-1894." See 378.

854 MC GURRIN, James. *Bourke Cochran*. See 173.

855 MC KELVEY, Blake. *Rochester: The Quest for Quality, 1890-1925*. Cambridge, Mass., 1956.

856 MAC RAE, Duncan, Jr., and James A. MELDRUM. "Critical Elections in Illinois, 1888-1958." *Am Pol Sci Rev*, LIV (1960), 669-683.

857 MC SEVENEY, Samuel Thompson. "The Politics of Depression: Voting Behavior in Connecticut, New York, and New Jersey, 1893-1896." Doctoral dissertation, University of Iowa, 1966.

858 MANDELBAUM, Seymour J. *Boss Tweed's New York.* New York, 1965.†

859 MANN, Arthur. *Yankee Reformers in the Urban Age.* Cambridge, Mass., 1954.

860 MARGULIES, Herbert F. *The Decline of the Progressive Movement in Wisconsin, 1890-1920.* Madison, 1968.

861 MAXWELL, Robert S. *La Follette and the Rise of Progressives in Wisconsin.* See 177.†

862 MERRILL, Horace Samuel. *Bourbon Democracy of the Middle West, 1865-1896.* See 750.†

863 MERRILL, Horace Samuel. *William Freeman Vilas.* See 178.

864 MILLER, Zane L. *Boss Cox's Cincinnati: Urban Politics in the Progressive Era.* New York, 1968.†

865 MOGER, Allen W. "The Origins of the Democratic Machine in Virginia." *J S Hist*, VIII (1942), 183-209.

866 MOGER, Allen W. *Virginia: Bourbonism to Byrd, 1870-1925.* Charlottesville, Va., 1968.

867 MOWRY, George E. *The California Progressives.* Berkeley, 1951.†

868 MYERS, Gustavus. *History of Tammany Hall.* New York, 1916.

869 NEVINS, Allan. *Grover Cleveland.* See 185.

870 NEVINS, Allan. *The Letters and Journals of Brand Whitlock.* See 280.

871 NEWCOMER, Lee. "Arthur's Removal from the Customs House." See 390.

872 NIELSON, James W. *Shelby M. Cullom.* See 187.

873 NOBLE, Ransom E., Jr. *New Jersey Progressivism Before Wilson.* Princeton, 1946.

874 NOYES, Edward. "The Ohio G. A. R. and Politics from 1866 to 1900." *Ohio State Arch Hist Q*, LV (1946), 79-105.

875 NYE, Russel B. *Midwestern Progressive Politics.* See 620.

876 OLIVER, John W. "Matthew Stanley Quay." See 191.

877 OLSON, James C. *J. Sterling Morton.* See 192.

878 OSTRANDER, Gilman Marston. *The Prohibition Movement in California, 1848-1933.* Berkeley, 1957.

879 PATTON, Clifford W. *The Battle for Municipal Reform: Mobilization and Attack, 1875-1900.* Washington, D.C., 1940.

880 PATTON, James W. "The Republican Party in South Carolina, 1876-1895." *Essays in Southern History Presented to Joseph Gregoire de Roulhac Hamilton.* Ed. Fletcher M. Green. Chapel Hill, 1949.

881 PEARSON, Charles Clinton. *The Readjuster Movement in Virginia.* New Haven, Conn., 1917.

882 PEARSON, Charles Clinton, and J. Edwin HENDRICKS. *Liquor and Anti-Liquor in Virginia, 1619-1919.* Durham, N.C., 1967.

883 PIERCE, Bessie Louise. *The Rise of a Modern City [Chicago], 1871-1893.* New York, 1957.

884 PLATT, Thomas Collier. *Autobiography.* See 287.

885 POMEROY, Earl S. *The Territories and the United States, 1861-1890: Studies in Colonial Administration.* Seattle, 1969.†

886 PULLEY, Raymond H. *Old Virginia Restored: An Interpretation of the Progressive Impulse, 1870-1930.* Charlottesville, Va., 1968.

887 RADER, Benjamin G. *The Academic Mind and Reform: The Influence of Richard T. Ely in American Life.* Lexington, Ky., 1966.

888 RAWLEY, James A. *Edwin D. Morgan.* See 196.

889 RICHARDSON, Leon Burr. *William E. Chandler.* See 197.

890 RIORDAN, William L. *Plunkitt of Tammany Hall.* See 199.

891 ROBISON, Daniel M. "From Tillman to Long: Some Striking Leaders of the New South." *J S Hist,* III (1937), 289-310.

892 SAGE, Leland L. *William Boyd Allison.* See 202.

893 SAXTON, Alexander. "San Francisco Labor and the Populist and Progressive Insurgencies." *Pac Hist Rev,* XXXIV (1965), 421-438.

894 SELLERS, James Benson. *The Prohibition Movement in Alabama, 1702 to 1943.* Chapel Hill, 1943.†

895 SIEVERS, Harry J. *Benjamin Harrison, Hoosier Statesman: 1865-1888.* See 205.

896 SIMKINS, Francis B. *Pitchfork Ben Tillman, South Carolinian.* See 206.†

897 SPROAT, John G. *"The Best Men": Liberal Reformers in the Gilded Age.* New York, 1968.†

898 STEELMAN, Joseph F. "The Progressive Era in North Carolina, 1884-1917." Doctoral dissertation, University of North Carolina, 1955.

899 STEFFENS, Lincoln. *The Shame of the Cities.* New York, 1904.†

900 STEFFENS, Lincoln. *The Struggle for Self-Government.* New York, 1906.

901 STEPHENSON, Nathaniel Wright. *Nelson W. Aldrich.* See 211.

902 SYRETT, Harold Coffin. *The City of Brooklyn, 1865-1898: A Political History.* New York, 1944.

903 TAGER, Jack. *The Intellectual as Urban Reformer: Brand Whitlock and the Progressive Movement.* See 214.

904 TARR, Joel A. "William Lorimer of Illinois." See 216.

905 TAYLOR, A. Elizabeth. *The Woman Suffrage Movement in Tennessee.* New York, 1957.

906 TAYLOR, A. Elizabeth. "The Women Suffrage Movement in Texas." *J S Hist*, XVII (1951), 194-215.

907 THELEN, David P. "The Social and Political Origins of Wisconsin Progressivism, 1885-1900." Doctoral dissertation, University of Wisconsin, 1967.

908 THELEN, David P. "Social Tensions and the Origins of Progressivism." *J Am Hist*, LVI (1969), 323-341.

909 TINSLEY, James A. "The Progressive Movement in Texas." Doctoral dissertation, University of Wisconsin, 1954.

910 TWETON, D. Jerome. "North Dakota in the 1890's: Its People, Politics, and Press." *ND Hist*, XXIV (1957), 113-118.

911 VAN DEUSEN, John G. "Did Republicans 'Colonize' Indiana in 1879?" See 427.

912 WAGONER, Jay J. *Arizona Territory, 1863-1912: A Political History.* Tucson, 1970.

913 WALTERS, Everett. *Joseph Benson Foraker.* See 220.

914 WARD, Judson C. "The Republican Party in Bourbon Georgia, 1872-1890." *J S Hist*, IX (1943), 196-209.

915 WARNER, Hoyt Landon. *Progressivism in Ohio, 1897-1917.* Columbus, Ohio, 1964.

916 WEISS, Nancy Joan. *Charles Francis Murphy, 1858-1924.* See 222.

917 WELCH, Richard E., Jr. "George Edmunds of Vermont." See 223.

918 WERNER, Morris R. *Tammany Hall.* New York, 1928.

919 WHITENER, Daniel J. *Prohibition in North Carolina, 1715-1945.* Chapel Hill, 1946.

920 WOODWARD, C. Vann. *Origins of the New South, 1877-1913.* See 710.†

921 YOUNGER, Edward. *John A. Kasson: Politics and Diplomacy from Lincoln to McKinley.* See 229.

922 ZINK, Harold. *City Bosses in the United States: A Study of Twenty Municipal Bosses.* Durham, N.C., 1930.

VII. Foreign Affairs

923 ADLER, Jacob. *Claus Spreckels: The Sugar King in Hawaii.* Honolulu, 1966.

924 ANGELL, James B. "The Diplomatic Relation between the United States and Japan." *J Soc Sci*, XVII (1883), 24-26.

925 ARMSTRONG, W. A. *E. L. Godkin and American Foreign Policy, 1865-1900.* New York, 1951.

926 BAILEY, Thomas A. "Japan's Protest against the Annexation of Hawaii." *J Mod Hist*, III (1931), 46-61.

927 BASTERT, Russell H. "Diplomatic Reversal: Frelinghuysen's Opposition to Blaine's Pan-American Policy in 1882." *Miss Val Hist Rev*, XLII (1955-1956), 653-671.

928 BASTERT, Russell H. "A New Approach to the Origins of Blaine's Pan-American Policy." *His-Am Hist Rev*, XXXIX (1959), 375-412.

929 BEISNER, Robert L. "Thirty Years before Manila: E. L. Godkin, Carl Schurz, and Anti-Imperialism in the Gilded Age." *Hist*, XXX (1968), 561-577.

930 BLAKE, Nelson M. "Background of Cleveland's Venezuela Policy." *Am Hist Rev*, XLVIII (1942), 259-277.

931 CAMPBELL, Alexander E. *Great Britain and the United States, 1895-1903.* London, 1960.

932 CAMPBELL, Charles S. *Anglo-American Understanding, 1898-1903.* Baltimore, 1957.

933 CARROLL, Edward J. "The Foreign Relations of the United States with Tsarist Russia 1867-1900." Doctoral dissertation, Georgetown University, 1953.

934 CURTI, Merle. "America at the World Fairs, 1851-1893." *Am Hist Rev*, LV (1950), 833-856.

935 DENNETT, Tyler. *Americans in Eastern Asia.* New York, 1922.

936 DENNETT, Tyler. *John Hay: From Poetry to Politics.* New York, 1933.

937 DENNIS, A. L. P. *Adventures in American Diplomacy, 1894-1907.* New York, 1928.

938 DOZER, Donald M. "Anti-Imperialism in the United States, 1865-1895." Doctoral dissertation, Harvard University, 1963.

939 DULLES, Foster Rhea. *China and America, the Story of Their Relations since 1784.* Princeton, 1946.

940 DULLES, Foster Rhea. *The Imperial Years.* New York, 1956.†

941 DULLES, Foster Rhea. *Prelude to World Power: American Diplomatic History, 1860-1900.* New York, 1965.

942 EDWARDS, Owen Dudley. "American Diplomats and Irish Coercion, 1880-1883." *J Am Stud*, I (1967), 213-232.

943 FOSTER, John W. *Diplomatic Memoirs.* See 256.

944 GELBER, Lionel M. *The Rise of Anglo-American Friendship: A Study in World Politics, 1898-1906.* London and New York, 1938.

945 GRENVILLE, John A. S., and George Berkeley YOUNG. *Politics, Strategy and American Diplomacy: Studies in Foreign Policy, 1873-1917.* New Haven, 1966.

946 GRISWOLD, Alfred Whitney. *The Far Eastern Policy of the United States.* New York, 1938.†

42 FOREIGN AFFAIRS

947 HARRINGTON, Fred H. *God, Mammon and the Japanese: Dr. Horace N. Allen and Korean-American Relations, 1884-1905.* Madison, 1944.

948 HAVEN, Gilbert. "America in Africa." *N Amer Rev*, CXXV (1887), 147-158.

949 HERRICK, Walter R., Jr. *The American Naval Revolution.* Baton Rouge, 1966.

950 HOLBO, Paul S. "Presidential Leadership in Foreign Affairs: William McKinley and the Turpie-Foraker Amendment." *Am Hist Rev*, LXXII (1967), 1321-1335.

951 KEIM, Jeanette. *Forty Years of German-American Political Relations.* Philadelphia, 1919.

952 LA FEBER, Walter. "The American Business Community and Cleveland's Venezuelan Message." *Bus Hist Rev*, XXXIV (1960), 393-402.

953 LA FEBER, Walter. "American Depression Diplomacy and the Brazilian Revolution, 1893-1894." *His-Am Hist Rev*, XL (1940), 107-118.

954 LA FEBER, Walter. "The Background of Cleveland's Venezuelan Policy: A Reinterpretation." *Am Hist Rev*, LXVI (1960-1961), 947-967.

955 LA FEBER, Walter. *The New Empire: An Interpretation of American Expansion 1860-1898.* Ithaca, N.Y., 1963.†

956 LANGLEY, Lester D. "The Democratic Tradition and Military Reform, 1878-1885." *S W Soc Sci Q*, XLVIII (1967), 192-200.

957 LIVEZEY, William E. *Mahan on Sea Power.* Norman, Okla., 1947.

958 MC CORMICK, Thomas J. *China Market: America's Quest for Informal Empire, 1893-1901.* Chicago, 1967.†

959 MC KEE, Delber Lee. "The American Federation of Labor and American Foreign Policy, 1886-1912." Doctoral dissertation, Stanford University, 1952.

960 MAHAN, Alfred T. *The Influence of Sea Power upon History 1660-1783.* Boston, 1890.†

961 MAHAN, Alfred T. *The Interest of America in Sea Power, Present and Future.* London, 1897.

962 MAHAN, Alfred T. "The United States Looking Outward." *Atl Mon*, LXVI (1890), 816-824.

963 MASTERMAN, Sylvia. *Origins of International Rivalry in Samoa, 1845-1884.* Stanford, 1934.

964 MATHEWS, Joseph J. "Informal Diplomacy in the Venezuela Crisis." *Miss Val Hist Rev*, L (1963), 195-212.

965 MAY, Ernest R. *American Imperialism: A Speculative Essay.* New York, 1968.

966 MAY, Ernest R. *Imperial Democracy, the Emergence of America as a Great Power.* New York, 1961.

967 MOON, Parker T. *Imperialism and World Politics.* New York, 1926.

968 NEUMANN, William L. *America Encounters Japan: From Perry to MacArthur.* Baltimore, 1963.†

969 NOBLE, Harold J. "The United States and Sino-Korean Relations, 1885-1887." *Pac Hist Rev*, II (1933), 292-304.

970 PAULIN, Charles O. "A Half Century of Naval Administration in America, 1861-1911." *Proc US Naval Inst*, XXXVIII (1912).

971 PERKINS, Bradford. *The Great Rapprochement: England and the United States, 1895-1914.* New York, 1968.

972 PERKINS, Dexter. *The Monroe Doctrine, 1867-1907.* Baltimore, 1937.†

973 PERKINS, Dexter. *The Monroe Doctrine, 1826-1867.* Gloucester, Mass., 1966.†

974 PLESUR, Milton. *America's Outward Thrust, Approaches to Foreign Affairs, 1865-1890.* DeKalb, Ill., 1971.†

975 PLESUR, Milton. "Rumblings beneath the Surface—America's Outward Thrust, 1865-1900." *The Gilded Age, A Reappraisal.* Ed. H. Wayne Morgan. Syracuse, 1963.†

976 PLETCHER, David M. *Foreign Policy under Garfield and Arthur.* See 399.

977 PRATT, Julius W. *America's Colonial Experiment.* New York, 1950.

978 PRATT, Julius W. *Expansionists of 1898: The Acquisition of Hawaii and the Spanish Islands.* Baltimore, 1936.†

979 PRATT, Julius W. "The Large Policy of 1898." *Miss Val Hist Rev*, XIX (1932), 219-242.

980 PULESTON, William D. *Mahan; the Life and Work of Captain Alfred Thayer Mahan.* New Haven, 1939.

981 QUINT, Howard H. "American Socialists and the Spanish-American War." *Am Q*, X (1958), 131-141.

982 RANDOLPH, Bessie Carter. "Foreign Bondholders and the Repudiated Debts of the Southern States." *Am J Int Law*, XXV (1931), 63-82.

983 ROTHSTEIN, Morton. "America in the International Rivalry for the British Wheat Market, 1860-1914." *Miss Val Hist Rev*, XL (1960), 401-418.

984 RUSS, William A., Jr. *The Hawaiian Republic, 1894-1898.* Selinsgrove, Pa., 1961.

985 RUSS, William A., Jr. *The Hawaiian Revolution, 1893-1894.* Selinsgrove, Pa., 1959.

986 RYDEN, George H. *The Foreign Policy of the United States in Relation to Samoa.* New Haven, 1933.

987 SEAGER, Robert, II. "Ten Years before Mahan: The Unofficial Case for the New Navy, 1880-1890." *Miss Val Hist Rev*, XL (1953), 491-512.

988 SKLAR, Martin J. "The NAM on the Eve of the Spanish-American War." *Sci Soc*, XXIII (1959), 133-162.

989 SNYDER. Louis L. "The American-German Pork Dispute, 1879-1881." *J Mod Hist*, XVII (1945), 16-28.

990 SPETTER, Allan. "Harrison and Blaine: Foreign Policy, 1889-1893." *Ind Mag Hist*, LXV (1969), 215-227.

991 SPROUT, Harold, and Margaret SPROUT. *The Rise of American Naval Power, 1776-1918*. Princeton, 1939.†

992 STEVENS, Sylvester K. *American Expansion in Hawaii, 1842-1898*. Harrisburg, Pa., 1945.

993 TANSILL, Charles Callan. *Canadian-American Relations, 1875-1911*. New York and Toronto, 1943.

994 TANSILL, Charles Callan. *The Foreign Policy of Thomas F. Bayard 1885-1897*. New York, 1940.

995 TATE, Merze. *The United States and the Hawaiian Kingdom*. New Haven, 1968.

996 THAYER, William R. *The Life and Letters of John Hay*. 2 vols. New York, 1908.

997 TOMPKINS, E. Berkeley. *Anti-Imperialism in the United States: The Great Debate, 1890-1920*. Philadelphia, 1970.

998 TREAT, Payson J. *Diplomatic Relations between the United States and Japan, 1853-1905*. 3 vols. Stanford, Calif., 1922-1928.

999 TYLER, Alice Felt. *Foreign Policy of Blaine*. See 426.

1000 VOLWILER, A. T. "Harrison, Blaine and Foreign Policy." *Proc Am Philos Soc*, LXXIX (1938), 637-648.

1001 WEINBERG, Albert K. *Manifest Destiny*. Baltimore, 1935.†

1002 WILGUS, A. C. "Blaine and the Pan-American Movement." *His-Am Hist Rev*, V (1922), 662-708.

1003 WILLIAMS, William Appleman. *The Roots of the Modern American Empire: A Study of the Growth and Shaping of Social Consciousness in a Marketplace Society*. New York, 1969.†

1004 WILLIAMS, William Appleman. *The Tragedy of American Diplomacy*. Rev. ed. New York, 1961.†

1005 YOUNG, Marilyn Blatt. *The Rhetoric of Empire: American China Policy, 1895-1901*. Cambridge, Mass., 1968.

VIII. Constitutional Developments

1006 BICKEL, Alexander M. "The Original Understanding and the Segregation Decision." *Har Law Rev*, LXIX (1955), 1-65.

1007 BOUDIN, Louis B. *Government by Judiciary*. 2 vols. New York, 1923.

1008 BOUDIN, Louis B. "Truth and Fiction about the Fourteenth Amendment." *N Y Univ Law Q Rev*, XVI (1938), 19-82.

1009 CORWIN, E. S. *Court Over Constitution*. Princeton, 1938.

1010 CUSHMAN, R. E. "The Social and Economic Interpretation of the Fourteenth Amendment." *Mich Law Rev*, XX (1922), 737-764.

1011 DANIELS, W. M. "Constitutional Growth under the Fourteenth Amendment." *S Atl Q*, XXIX (1930), 16-34.

1012 EGGERT, Gerald G. "Richard Olney and the Income Tax Cases." *Miss Val Hist Rev*, XLVIII (1961), 24-41.

1013 FAIRMAN, Charles. *Mr. Justice Miller and the Supreme Court, 1862-1890.* Cambridge, Mass., 1939.

1014 FAIRMAN, Charles. "The So-Called Granger Cases, Lord Hale, and Justice Bradley." *Stan Law Rev*, V (1953), 587-679.

1015 FRANKFURTER, Felix, and N. V. GREENE. *The Labor Injunction.* New York, 1930.

1016 FREUND, Ernst. *The Police Power.* Chicago, 1904.

1017 GRAHAM, Howard Jay. *Everyman's Constitution: Historical Essays on the Fourteenth Amendment, the "Conspiracy Theory," and American Constitutionalism.* Madison, 1968.

1018 GRAHAM, Howard Jay. "Our 'Declaratory' Fourteenth Amendment." *Stan Law Rev*, VII (1954), 3-39.

1019 "The Granger Decisions." *Nation*, XXIV (March 8, 1877), 143-144.

1020 GROAT, G. C. *Attitude of American Courts in Labor Cases.* New York, 1911.

1021 HAINES, Charles G. "The History of Due Process after the Civil War." *Selected Essays on Constitutional Law*, I. Ed. Association of American Law Schools. Chicago, 1938.

1022 HAINES, Charles G. "Judicial Review of Legislation in the United States and the Doctrine of Vested Rights." *Tex Law Rev*, II (1924), 257-290, 387-421; III (1924), 1-43.

1023 HAMILTON, Walter H. "The Path of Due Process of Law." *The Constitution Reconsidered.* Ed. Conyers Read. New York, 1938.

1024 HOLMES, Oliver Wendell, Jr. *The Common Law.* Boston, 1881.†

1025 HOWE, Mark A. De Wolfe. *Justice Oliver Wendell Holmes: The Proving Years, 1870-1882.* Cambridge, Mass., 1963.

1026 KELLY, Alfred H., and Winfred A. HARBISON. *The American Constitution.* 3d ed. New York, 1963.

1027 KELLY, Alfred H. "The Congressional Controversy over School Segregation, 1867-1875." *Am Hist Rev*, LXIV (1959), 537-563.

1028 KELLY, Alfred H. "The Fourteenth Amendment Reconsidered: The Segregation Question." *Mich Law Rev*, LIV (1956), 1049-1086.

1029 KING, Willard L. *Melville Weston Fuller: Chief Justice of the United States, 1888-1910.* New York, 1910.†

1030 LERNER, Max, ed. *The Mind and the Faith of Justice Holmes.* New York, 1943.

1031 LEVY, Leonard. "Chief Justice Shaw and the Formative Period of Railway Law." *Colum Law Rev*, LI (1951), 852-865.

1032 LEVY, Leonard, and H. B. PHILLIPS. "The Roberts Case: Source of the Separate but Equal Doctrine." *Am Hist Rev*, LVI (1951), 510–518.

1033 MC CLOSKEY, Robert Green. *The American Supreme Court*. Chicago, 1960.†

1034 MC LAUGHLIN, A. C. *A Constitutional History of the United States*. New York, 1935.

1035 MC LAUGHLIN, A. C. "Court, Corporation and Conkling." *Am Hist Rev*, XLVI (1940), 45–63.

1036 MAGRATH, C. Peter. *Morrison R. Waite: The Triumph of Character*. New York, 1963.

1037 MASON, Alpheus T. *Brandeis: A Free Man's Life*. New York, 1946.

1038 MILLER, George H. "Origins of the Iowa Granger Law." *Miss Val Hist Rev*, XL (1954), 657–680.

1039 PAUL, Arnold M. *Conservative Crisis and the Rule of Law: Attitudes of Bar and Bench, 1887–1895*. Ithaca, N.Y., 1960.†

1040 POUND, Roscoe. "Liberty of Contract." *Yale Law J*, XVIII (1909), 454–487.

1041 RATNER, Sidney. *American Taxation*. New York, 1942.

1042 RUSSELL, James F. "The Railroads and the Conspiracy Theory of the Fourteenth Amendment." *Miss Val Hist Rev*, XLI (1955), 601–622.

1043 SHATTUCK, C. E. "The True Meaning of the Term 'Liberty' in Those Clauses in the Federal and State Constitutions which Protect Life, Liberty, and Property." *Har Law Rev*, IV (1891), 364–392.

1044 SWINDLER, William F. *Court and Constitution in the Twentieth Century: The Old Legality, 1889–1932*. Indianapolis and New York, 1969.

1045 SWISHER, Carl B. *American Constitutional Development*. Boston, 1943.

1046 SWISHER, Carl B. *Stephen J. Field; Craftsman of the Law*. Washington, 1930.†

1047 TRIMBLE, Bruce R. *Chief Justice Waite, Defender of the Public Interest*. Princeton, 1938.

1048 WARREN, Charles. "The New 'Liberty' under the Fourteenth Amendment." *Har Law Rev*, XXXIX (1926), 431–465.

1049 WARREN, Charles. *The Supreme Court in United States History*. Boston, 1926.

1050 WEISENBURGER, Francis Phelps. *The Life of John McLean, a Politician on the United States Supreme Court*. Columbus, Ohio, 1937.

IX. Civil Service Reform

1051 CARY, Edward. *George Williams Curtis.* See 108.

1052 FISH, Carl R. *The Civil Service and the Patronage.* Cambridge, Mass., 1920.

1053 FOULKE, William Dudley. *Fighting the Spoilsmen; Reminiscences of the Civil Service Reform Movement.* See 257.

1054 FUESS, Claude Moore. *Carl Schurz.* See 130.

1055 GOSNELL, Harold. *Boss Platt and His New York Machine.* See 139.

1056 HARTMAN, William J. "Politics and Patronage: The New York Customs House, 1852-1902." Doctoral dissertation, Columbia University, 1952.

1057 HOOGENBOOM, Ari. "An Analysis of Civil Service Reformers." *Hist,* XXIII (1960), 54-78.

1058 HOOGENBOOM, Ari. *Outlawing the Spoils: A History of the Civil Service Reform Movement.* Urbana, Ill., 1961.

1059 HOOGENBOOM, Ari. "The Pendleton Act and the Civil Service." *Am Hist Rev,* LXIV (1959), 301-318.

1060 HOOGENBOOM, Ari. "Spoilsmen and Reformers, Civil Service Reform and Public Morality." *The Gilded Age, a Reappraisal.* Ed. H. Wayne Morgan. Syracuse, 1963.

1061 HOOGENBOOM, Ari. "Thomas A. Jenckes and Civil Service Reform." *Miss Val Hist Rev,* XLVII (1961), 636-658.

1062 LAMBERT, Henry. *The Progress of the Civil Service Reform in the United States.* Boston, 1885.

1063 MC FARLAND, Gerald. "Partisan of Nonpartisanship: Dorman B. Eaton and the Genteel Reform Tradition." *J Amer Hist,* LIV (1968), 806-822.

1064 MERRIAM, George S. *The Life and Times of Samuel Bowles.* 2 vols. New York, 1885.

1065 MILNE, Gordon. *George William Curtis and the Genteel Tradition.* See 180.

1066 NORTON, Charles Eliot, ed. *Orations and Addresses of George William Curtis.* See 282.

1067 OGDEN, Rollo. *Life and Letters of Godkin.* See 189.

1068 RIORDON, William L. *Plunkitt of Tammany Hall.* See 199.†

1069 SAGESER, Adelbert B. *The First Two Decades of the Pendleton Act; a Study of Civil Service Reform.* Lincoln, Neb., 1935.

1070 SMITH, Darrell H. *The United States Civil Service Commission; Its History, Activities and Organization.* Baltimore, 1928.

1071 SPROAT, John G. *"The Best Men": Liberal Reformers in the Gilded Age.* See 897.†

1072 STEWART, Frank M. *The National Civil Service Reform League: History, Activities and Problems.* Austin, 1929.

1073 THATCHER, John Howard. "Public Discussion of Civil Service Reform, 1864-1883." Doctoral dissertation, Cornell University, 1943.

1074 VAN RIPER, R. P. *History of the United States Civil Service.* Evanston, Ill., 1958.

1075 WALL, Joseph Frazier. *Henry Watterson.* See 219.

1076 WHITE, Leonard D. *The Republican Era.* See 91.

X. Currency Question

1077 ANDREWS, Elisha Benjamin. *An Honest Dollar.* Hartford, Conn., 1894.

1078 BARNES, James A. *John G. Carlisle.* See 97.

1079 BARNETT, Paul. *Business Cycle Theory in the United States, 1860-1900.* Chicago, 1941.

1080 BARRETT, D. C. *The Greenbacks and the Resumption of Specie Payment, 1862-1879.* Cambridge, Mass., 1931.

1081 BURTON, T. E. *Financial Crises and Periods of Industrial and Commercial Depression.* New York, 1908.†

1082 CLEWS, Henry. *Fifty Years in Wall Street.* New York, 1908.

1083 CORNWALL, William G. *Free Coinage from the Businessman's Standpoint.* See 496.

1084 DESTLER, Chester M. "The Origin and Character of the Pendleton Plan." *Miss Val Hist Rev,* XXIV (1937), 171-184.

1085 DEWEY, Davis R. *Financial History of the United States.* 10th ed. New York, 1928.

1086 DONNELLY, Ignatius. *The American People's Money.* Chicago, 1895.

1087 ECKLER, A. Ross. "A Measure of the Severity of the Depression, 1873-1932." *Rev Econ Stat,* XV (1933), 75-81.

1088 EDWARDS, George W. *The Evolution of Finance Capitalism.* New York, 1938.

1089 ELLIS, Elmer. *Henry Moore Teller.* See 127.

1090 FISHER, Willard C. "Coin and His Critics." *Q J Econ,* X (1896), 187-208.

1091 FRIEDMAN, Milton, and A. J. SCHWARTZ. *A Monetary History of the United States 1867-1920.* Princeton, 1963.†

1092 HARVEY, William H. *Coin's Financial School.* Chicago, 1894.†

1093 HARVEY, William H. *Up to Date, Coin's Financial School Continued.* Chicago, 1895.

1094 HEPBURN, Alonzo B. *A History of Currency in the United States.* New York, 1915.

1095 HOFFMAN, Charles. "The Depression of the Nineties." *J Econ Hist.* See 361.

1096 HOFFMAN, Charles. "The Depression of the Nineties—An Economic History." Doctoral dissertation, Columbia University, 1954.

1097 JOHNSON, Claudius O. "The Story of Silver Politics in Idaho, 1892-1902." *Pac N W Q,* XXXIII (1942), 283-296.

1098 LARSON, Henrietta M. *Jay Cooke.* Cambridge, Mass., 1936.

1099 LAUGHLIN, James Laurence. *History of Bimetallism in United States.* 4th ed. New York, 1897.

1100 NICHOLS, Jeannette P. "John Sherman and the Silver Drive of 1877-1878." *Ohio State Arch Hist Q.* See 393.

1101 NOYES, Alexander D. *Forty Years of American Finance, 1865-1907.* New York, 1909.

1102 NUGENT, Walter T. K. *Money and American Society, 1865-1880.* New York, 1968.

1103 OBERHOLTZER, Ellis P. *Jay Cooke.* 2 vols. Philadelphia, 1907.

1104 REDLICH, Fritz. *The Molding of American Banking: Men and Ideas.* Part II, 1840-1910. New York, 1951.

1105 RUGGLES, Clyde O. "The Economic Basis of the Greenback Movement in Iowa and Wisconsin." *Proc Miss Val Hist Assoc,* VI (1912-1913), 142-165.

1106 RUSSELL, Henry B. *International Monetary Conferences, Their Purposes, Character and Results.* New York, 1898.

1107 SCHULTZ, William J., and M. R. CAINE. *Financial Development of the United States.* New York, 1937.

1108 SHIPLEY, Max L. "The Background and Legal Aspects of the Pendleton Plan." *Miss Val Hist Rev,* XXIV (1937), 329-340.

1109 SPRAGUE, O. M. W. *History of Crises under the National Banking System.* Washington, D.C., 1910.

1110 STUDENSKI, Paul, and Herman E. KROOS. *Financial History of the United States.* New York, 1952.

1111 TAUS, Esther R. *Central Banking Functions of the United States Treasury, 1789-1941.* New York, 1943.

1112 TAUSSIG, Frank W. *The Silver Situation in the United States. Pub Am Econ Assoc,* VII (1892), 1-118.

1113 UNGER, Irwin. "Businessmen and Specie Resumption." *Pol Sci Q,* LXXIV (1959), 46-70.

1114 UNGER, Irwin. *The Greenback Era, a Social and Political History of American Finance 1865-1879.* Princeton, 1964.

1115 USHER, Ellis B. *The Greenback Movement of 1875-1884 and Wisconsin's Part in It.* Milwaukee, 1911.

1116 WALKER, Francis A. "The Free Coinage of Silver." See 688.

1117 WALKER, Francis A. *International Bimetallism*. New York, 1896.

1118 WEINSTEIN, Allan. *Prelude to Populism: Origins of the Silver Issue, 1867-1878*. New Haven, 1970.

1119 WELLBORN, Fred. "The Influence of the Silver-Republican Senators, 1889-1891." *Miss Val Hist Rev*. See 433.

XI. Tariff Question

1120 COLE, Arthur N. *The American Wool Industry*. Cambridge, Mass., 1926.

1121 FRIEDMAN, Milton, and A. J. SCHWARTZ. *A Monetary History of the United States*. See 1091.†

1122 GEORGE, Henry. *Protection or Free Trade?* New York, 1886.

1123 JOYNER, F. B. *David A. Wells: Champion of Free Trade*. Cedar Rapids, Iowa, 1939.

1124 LAUGHLIN, James L., and H. Parker WILLIS. *Reciprocity*. New York, 1903.

1125 MILLER, Clarence L. *The States of the Old Northwest and the Tariff, 1865-1888*. Emporia, Kan., 1929.

1126 MILLS, Roger Q. "The Wilson Bill." *N Amer Rev*, CLVIII (1894), 235-244.

1127 OSBORNE, John B. "The Work of the Reciprocity Commission." *Forum*. XXX (1900), 394-411.

1128 ROBINSON, Chalfont. *A History of Two Reciprocity Treaties*. New Haven, 1904.

1129 STANWOOD, Edward. *American Tariff Controversies of the Nineteenth Century*. 2 vols. Boston, 1903.

1130 SUMMERS, Festus P. *William L. Wilson and Tariff Reform*. See 213.

1131 TARBELL, Ida. *The Tariff in Our Times*. New York, 1911.

1132 TAUSSIG, Frank W. *Some Aspects of the Tariff Question*. Cambridge, Mass., 1915.

1133 TAUSSIG, Frank W. *The Tariff History of the United States*. 7th ed. New York, 1923.

1134 TERRILL, Tom E. "David A. Wells, the Democracy, and Tariff Reduction, 1877-1894." *J Am Hist*, LVI (1969), 540-555.

1135 VOLWILER, A. T. "Tariff Strategy and Propaganda in the United States, 1887-1888." *Am Hist Rev*, XXXVI (1930), 76-96.

1136 WELLS, David A. *Relation of Tariff to Wages*. New York, 1888.

1137 WRIGHT, Chester W. *Wool Growing and the Tariff: A Study in the Economic History of the United States*. Cambridge, Mass., 1910.

XII. Trust and Monopoly Question

1138 ALLEN, Frederick L. *The Great Pierpont Morgan.* New York, 1949.†

1139 ALLEN, Frederick L. *The Lords of Creation.* New York, 1935.†

1140 BELLAMY, Edward. *Looking Backward; 2000-1887.* Boston and New York, 1888.†

1141 BERGLAND, A. "The United States Steel Corporation." *Stud Hist Econ Pub Law* (Colum), XXVII, No. 2 (1907).

1142 BRIDGE, James H. *The Trust: Its Book.* New York, 1902.

1143 CLARK, John D. *The Federal Trust Policy.* London, 1931.

1144 CONANT, Luther. "Industrial Consolidation in the United States." *Pub Am Stat Assn,* VII, No. 53 (1901).

1145 COOK, William W. *The Corporation Problem.* New York, 1891.

1146 COREY, Lewis. *The House of Morgan: A Social Biography of the Masters of Money.* New York, 1930.

1147 DEWING, Arthur S. *Corporate Promotions and Reorganizations.* Cambridge, Mass., 1914.

1148 DUNBAR, William H. "State Regulation of Prices and Rates." *Q J Econ,* IX (1895), 305-332.

1149 GEORGE, Henry. *Progress and Poverty.* San Francisco, 1879.†

1150 HEAD, Franklin, ed. *Chicago Conference on Trusts.* Chicago, 1900.

1151 HUNTER, Louis C. "Studies in the Economic History of the Ohio Valley: The Beginnings of Industrial Combinations." *Stud Hist* (Smith), XIX, Nos. 1-2. Northampton, Mass., 1934.

1152 HURST, J. W. *Law and the Conditions of Freedom in the Nineteenth-Century United States.* Madison, 1956.†

1153 JACOBSTEIN, Meyer. "The Tobacco Industry." *Stud Hist Econ Pub Law* (Colum), XXVI, No. 3 (1907).

1154 JAMES, Edmund J. "Agitation for Federal Regulation." *Pub Am Econ Assn,* II (1887-1888), 236-267.

1155 JENKS, Jermiah W., and Walter E. CLARK. *The Trust Problem.* 4th ed. Garden City, N.Y., 1917.

1156 JONES, Eliot. *The Anthracite Coal Combination in the United States.* Cambridge, Mass., 1914.

1157 JONES, Eliot. *The Trust Problem in the United States.* New York, 1921.

1158 KEEZER, Dexter M., and Stacy MAY. *The Public Control of Business.* New York, 1930.

1159 KNAUTH, Oswald W. *The Policy of the United States towards Industrial Monopoly.* New York, 1914.

1160 LAIDLER, Harry W. *Concentration of Control in American Industry.* New York, 1931.

1161 LEWTIN, William. *Law and Economic Policy in America: The Evolution of the Sherman Anti-Trust Law.* New York, 1965.

1162 MESSEY, Henry R. "Combination in the Mining Industry; a Study of Concentration in Lake Superior Iron Ore Production." *Stud Hist Econ Pub Law* (Colum), XXIII, No. 3 (1905).

1163 MOODY, John. *The Masters of Capital.* New Haven, 1921.

1164 MOODY, John. *The Truth about the Trusts.* Chicago, 1904.

1165 RIPLEY, William Z. *Trusts, Pools, and Corporations.* Boston and New York, 1905.

1166 SEAGER, Henry R. "The Recent Trust Decisions." *Pol Sci Q,* XXVI (1911), 581-614.

1167 SEAGER, Henry R., and Charles A. GULICK. *Trust and Corporation Problems.* New York and London, 1929.

1168 STEVENS, William S. "A Classification of Pools and Associations Based on American Experience." *Am Econ Rev,* III (1913), 545-575.

1169 STEVENS, William S. "A Group of Trusts and Combinations." *Q J Econ,* XXVI (1912), 593-643.

1170 THORELLI, Hans B. *The Federal Anti-Trust Policy: Organization of an American Tradition.* Baltimore, 1955.

1171 VAN HISE, Charles R. *Concentration and Control; A Solution of the Trust Problem in the United States.* Rev. ed. New York, 1914.

1172 WALKER, Albert H. *History of the Sherman Law of the United States of America.* New York, 1910.

1173 WASHBURN, C. G. "Sherman Antitrust Act." *Bos Univ Law Rev,* VIII (1928), 95-116.

1174 WATKINS, Myron W. *Industrial Combinations and Public Policy; a Study of Combination, Competition and the Common Welfare.* Boston and New York, 1927.

1175 WILLOUGHBY, William Franklin. "Concentration of Industry." *Yale Rev,* VII (1898), 72-94.

1176 WILLOUGHBY, William Franklin. "Integration of Industry." *Q J Econ,* XVI (1902), 94-115.

XIII. The Rise of Industry

1. General

1177 BARGER, Harold. *Distribution's Place in the American Economy.* Princeton, 1955.

1178 BARNETT, Paul. *Business Cycle Theory in the United States, 1860-1900.* Chicago, 1941.

1179 BURLINGAME, Roger. *Engines of Democracy; Inventions and Society in Mature America.* New York, 1940.

1180 BYRN, Edward W. *The Progress of Invention in the Nineteenth Century.* New York, 1900.

1181 CHAMBERLAIN, John. *The Enterprising Americans.* New York, 1963.†

1182 CHANDLER, Alfred D., Jr. "The Beginnings of 'Big Business' in American Industry." *Bus Hist Rev,* XXXIII (1959), 1-31.

1183 CHANDLER, Alfred D., Jr. *Strategy and Structure; Chapters in the History of the American Industrial Enterprise.* Cambridge, Mass., 1962.†

1184 CLARK, V. S. *History of Manufacturers in the United States, 1860-1893.* New York, 1929.

1185 COCHRAN, Thomas C., and William MILLER. *The Age of Enterprise: A History of Industrial America.* New York, 1942.†

1186 DERBER, Milton. *The American Idea of Industrial Democracy.* Urbana, Ill., 1970.

1187 DIAMOND, Sigmund, ed. *The Nation Transformed: The Creation of Industrial Society.* New York, 1963.†

1188 DORFMAN, Joseph. *The Economic Mind in American Civilization, 1865-1918.* New York, 1949.

1189 EDWARDS, George W. *The Evolution of Finance Capitalism.* London and New York, 1938.

1190 EVANS, G. Heberton, Jr. *Business Incorporation in the United States; 1800-1943.* New York, 1948.

1191 EVANS, G. Heberton, Jr. "A Century of Entrepreneurship in the United States with Emphasis upon Large Manufacturing Concerns." *Explorations in Entrepreneurial History,* X (1957), 90-103.

1192 FELS, Rendig. *American Business Cycles, 1865-1897.* Chapel Hill, 1959.

1193 FELS, Rendig. "American Business Cycles, 1865-79." *Am Econ Rev,* XLI (1951), 325-349.

1194 FRICKLEY, Edwin. *Production in the United States: 1860-1914.* Cambridge, Mass., 1947.

1195 FRIEDMAN, Milton, and A. J. SCHWARTZ. *A Monetary History of the United States, 1867-1960.* See 1091.†

1196 HABAKKUK, H. J. *American and British Technology in the Nineteenth Century.* Cambridge, Eng., 1962.†

1197 HANSEN, A. H. *Business Cycles and National Income.* New York, 1964.

1198 HENDRICK, Burton J. *The Age of Big Business; a Chronicle of the Captains of Industry.* New Haven, 1919.

1199 HOFSTADTER, Richard. *Social Darwinism in American Thought.* Rev. ed. New York, 1959.†

1200 KAEMPFFERT, Waldemar, ed. *A Popular History of American Inventions.* 2 vols. New York, 1924.

1201 KEIR, Malcolm. *Manufacturing Industries in America; Fundamental Economic Factors.* New York, 1920.

1202 KIRKLAND, Edward C. *Business in the Gilded Age: The Conservatives' Balance Sheet.* Madison, 1952.

1203 KIRKLAND, Edward C. *Dream and Thought in the Business Community, 1860-1900.* Ithaca, N.Y., 1953.†

1204 KIRKLAND, Edward C. *Industry Comes of Age. Business, Labor and Public Policy, 1860-1897.* New York, 1961.†

1205 KUZNETS, Simon. *National Income: A Summary of Findings.* New York, 1946.

1206 LIVELY, Robert A. "The American System." *Bus Hist Rev*, XXIX (1955), 81-96.

1207 MUMFORD, Lewis. *Technics and Civilization.* New York, 1934.†

1208 NAVIN, Thomas R., and Marian V. SEARS. "The Rise of a Market for Industrial Securities." *Bus Hist Rev*, XXIX (1955), 105-138.

1209 NEVINS, Allan. *The Emergence of Modern America.* New York, 1927.

1210 NORTH, D. C. *Growth and Welfare in the American Economy.* Englewood Cliffs, N.J., 1966.

1211 OLIVER, John W. *History of American Technology.* New York, 1956.

1212 STRASSMANN, W. P. *Risk and Technological Innovation: American Manufacturing Methods during the Nineteenth Century.* Ithaca, N.Y., 1959.

1213 TARBELL, Ida M. *The Nationalizing of Business 1878-1898.* New York, 1936.

1214 USHER, A. P. *A History of Mechanical Inventions.* Cambridge, Mass., 1954.

1215 VEBLEN, Thorstein. *Absentee Ownership and Business Enterprise in Recent Times; the Case of America.* New York, 1923.†

1216 WELLS, David A. *Recent Economic Changes.* New York, 1889.

1217 WILLIAMSON, Harold F., ed. *Growth of the American Economy.* 2d ed. New York, 1951.

1218 WOOD, J. P. *The Story of Advertising.* New York, 1958.

1219 WRIGHT, C. D. *The Industrial Evolution of the United States.* New York, 1897.

2. Industries

1220 ALLEN, Frederick J. *The Shoe Industry.* New York, 1922.

1221 ARMES, Ethel. *The Story of Coal and Iron in Alabama.* Birmingham, 1910.

1222 ARNOLD, John P., and Frank PENMAN. *History of Brewing Industry and Brewing Science in America.* Chicago, 1933.

1223 BAER, Willis. *The Economic Development of the Cigar Industry in the United States.* Lancaster, Pa., 1933.

1224 BRIDGE, James H. *Inside History of the Carnegie Steel Company; a Romance of Millions.* New York, 1903.

1225 BRIGHT, Arthur A., Jr. *The Electric-Lamp Industry.* New York, 1949.

1226 BURN, D. L. *Economic History of Steelmaking.* Cambridge, Eng., 1940.

1227 BUTLER, Joseph G. *Fifty Years of Iron and Steel.* Cleveland, 1923.

1228 CASSON, Herbert. *The Romance of Steel; the Story of a Thousand Millionaires.* New York, 1907.

1229 CLARK, Joseph Stanley. *The Oil Century: From the Drake Well to the Conservation Era.* Norman, Okla., 1958.

1230 CLELAND, Robert G. *A History of Phelps Dodge, 1834-1950.* New York, 1952.

1231 COCHRAN, Thomas C. *The Pabst Brewing Company.* New York, 1948.

1232 COLE, Arthur H. *The American Wool Manufacture.* 2 vols. Cambridge, Mass., 1926.

1233 COLLINS, James H. *The Story of Canned Foods.* New York, 1924.

1234 COPELAND, M. T. *The Cotton Manufacturing Industry in the United States.* Cambridge, Mass., 1912.

1235 DUTTON, William S. *DuPont; One Hundred and Forty Years.* New York, 1942.

1236 EATON, Amasa M. "Oil Regions of Pennsylvania, 1865." *W Pa Hist Mag,* XVIII (1935), 189-208.

1237 GALAMBOS, Louis. "The Agrarian Image of the Large Corporation, 1869-1920." See 540.

1238 GANNON, Frederic A. *Shoemaking, Old and New.* Salem, Mass., 1912.

1239 GATES, William B. *Michigan Copper and Boston Dollars: An Economic History of the Michigan Copper Mining Industry.* Cambridge, Mass., 1951.

1240 GIBB, George S. *The Saco-Lowell Shops: Textile Machinery Building in New England, 1813-1949.* Cambridge, Mass., 1950.

1241 GIDDENS, Paul H. *The Birth of the Oil Industry.* New York, 1938.

1242 GIDDENS, Paul H. *Pennsylvania Petroleum, 1750-1872, a Documentary.* Titusville, Pa., 1947.†

1243 GIDDENS, Paul H. *Standard Oil Company (Indiana): Oil Pioneer of the Middle West.* New York, 1956.

1244 GLAAB, Charles N., and Lawrence H. LARSEN. *Factories in the Valley: Neenah-Menasha [Wis.], 1870-1915.* Madison, 1969.

1245 HIDY, Ralph W., and M. E. HIDY. *History of Standard Oil Company (New Jersey): Pioneering in Big Business, 1882-1911.* New York, 1955.

1246 HOTCHKISS, George W. *History of the Lumber and Forest Industry of the Northwest.* Chicago, 1898.

1247 HOWER, R. M. *History of Macy's of New York, 1858-1919: Chapters in the Evolution of the Department Store.* Cambridge, Mass., 1943.

1248 HUNTER, Louis C. *Steamboats on the Western Rivers. An Economic and Technological History.* Cambridge, Mass., 1949.

1249 HURST, James Willard. *The Legitimacy of the Business Corporation in the Law of the United States, 1780-1970.* Charlottesville, Va., 1970.

1250 JOHNSON, A. M. *The Development of American Petroleum Pipelines: A Study in Private Enterprise and Public Policy, 1862-1906.* Ithaca, N.Y., 1956.

1251 KELLER, Morton. *The Life Insurance Enterprise, 1885-1910: A Study in the Limits of Corporate Power.* Cambridge, Mass., 1963.

1252 LAWRENCE, Albert A. *Petroleum Comes of Age.* Tulsa, Okla., 1938.

1253 MEADE, E. S. "The Genesis of the United States Steel Corporation." *Q J Econ,* XV (1901), 532-541.

1254 MITCHELL, Broadus. *The Rise of Cotton Mills in the South.* Baltimore, 1921.

1255 MONTAGUE, Gilbert H. *The Rise and Progress of the Standard Oil Company.* New York and London, 1903.

1256 NAVIN, T. R. *The Whitin Machine Works since 1831: A Textile Machinery Company in an Industrial Village.* Cambridge, Mass., 1950.

1257 PASSER, Harold C. *The Electrical Manufacturers, 1875-1900: A Study in Competition, Entrepreneurship, Technical Change and Economic Growth.* Cambridge, Mass., 1953.

1258 PIRTLE, Thomas R. *History of the Dairy Industry.* Chicago, 1926.

1259 RUSSELL, Charles Edward. *The Greatest Trust in the World.* New York, 1905.

1260 SMITH, Joseph R. *The Story of Iron and Steel.* New York, 1908.

1261 TAIT, Samuel W., Jr. *The Wild Catters: An Informal History of Oil Hunting in America.* Princeton, 1946.

1262 TARBELL, Ida M. *History of the Standard Oil Company.* 2 vols. New York, 1904.†

1263 TEMIN, Peter. *Iron and Steel in Nineteenth Century America: An Economic Inquiry.* Cambridge, Mass., 1964.

1264 THORNTON, Harrison J. *The History of the Quaker Oats Company.* Chicago, 1933.

1265 VOGT, Paul L. *Sugar Refining Industry in the United States.* Philadelphia, 1908.

1266 WERTIME, T. A. *The Coming of the Age of Steel.* Chicago, 1962.

1267 WIEST, Edward. *Butter Industry in the United States; an Economic Study of Butter and Oleomargarine.* New York, 1916.

1268 WILLIAMSON, Harold F., et al. *The American Petroleum Industry 1859-1899: The Age of Illumination.* Evanston, Ill., 1959.

1269 WINCHELL, Newton H., and H. V. WINCHELL. *The Discovery and Development of the Iron Ores of Minnesota.* St. Paul, 1891.

1270 WINKLER, John K. *Du Pont Dynasty.* New York, 1935.

1271 WIRTH, Fremont P. *The Discovery and Exploitation of the Minnesota Iron Lands.* Cedar Rapids, Iowa, 1937.

1272 WOLBERT, George S., Jr. *American Pipe Lines, Their Industrial Structure, Economic Status, and Legal Implications.* Norman, Okla., 1952.

1273 WOODRUFF, Ruth J. "American Hosiery Industry, 1873-1895, with Special Reference to the Downward Trend of Prices." *J Econ Bus Hist,* IV (1931), 18-37.

3. Railroads

1274 ADAMS, Charles Francis, Jr. *Railroads: Their Origins and Problems.* New York, 1879.

1275 *Annual Reports and Statistics of Railways in the United States.* Published annually since 1888 by Interstate Commerce Commission.

1276 BEARD, E. S. "The Background of State Regulation in Iowa." *Iowa J Hist,* LI (1953), 1-36.

1277 BEARD, E. S. "Local Aid to Railroads in Iowa." *Iowa J Hist,* L (1952), 1-34.

1278 BENSON, Lee. *Merchants, Farmers, and Railroads: Railroad Regulation and New York Politics, 1850-1887.* See 772.

1279 BOGEN, Jules I. *The Anthracite Railroads.* New York, 1927.

1280 BONBRIGHT, James C. *Railroad Capitalization.* New York, 1920.

1281 BRADLEY, G. D. *Santa Fe.* Boston, 1920.

1282 BUNTING, J. W. *The Distance Principle in Railroad Rate Making.* Geneva, N.Y., 1947.

1283 BURGESS, George H., and Miles C. KENNEDY. *Centennial History of the Pennsylvania Railroad Company.* Philadelphia, 1949.

1284 CAMPBELL, Edward Gross. "Indebted Railroad, a Problem of Reconstruction." *J S Hist,* VI (1940), 167-188.

1285 CAMPBELL, Edward Gross. *The Reorganization of the American Railroad System, 1893-1900.* New York, 1938.

1286 CARMAN, Harry J., and Charles H. MUELLER. "Contract and Finance Corporation and Central Pacific." *Miss Val Hist Rev,* XIV (1927), 326-341.

1287 CARY, John W. *The Organization and History of the Chicago, Milwaukee and St. Paul Railway Company.* Milwaukee, 1892.

1288 CHANDLER, Alfred D., Jr., ed. *The Railroads, the Nation's First Big Business: Sources and Readings.* New York, 1965.†

1289 CLARK, George T. *Leland Stanford, War Governor of California, Railroad Builder and Founder of Stanford University.* Stanford, 1931.

1290 CLEVELAND, Frederick A., and Fred W. POWELL. *Railroad Promotion and Capitalization in the United States.* New York, 1909.

1291 COCHRAN, Thomas C. "Land Grants and Railroad Entrepreneurship." *J Econ Hist,* X (1950), Suppl., 53-67.

1292 COMBS, Barry B. "The Union Pacific Railroad and the Early Settlement of Nebraska, 1868-1880." *Neb Hist,* L (1969), 1-26.

1293 COREY, Lewis. *The House of Morgan: A Social Biography of the Masters of Money.* See 1146.

1294 DAGGETT, Stuart. *Chapters on the History of the Southern Pacific.* New York, 1922.

1295 DAGGETT, Stuart. *Railroad Reorganization.* Cambridge, Mass., 1908.

1296 DALAND, R. T. "Enactment of the Potter Law." *Wis Mag Hist,* XXXIII (1949), 45-54.

1297 DECKER, L. E. *Railroads, Lands and Politics: The Taxation of the Railroad Land Grants, 1864-1897.* Providence, 1964.

1298 DIXON, Frank H. "Railroad Control in Nebraska." *Pol Sci Q,* XIII (1898), 617-647.

1299 DIXON, Frank H. *Railroads and Government.* New York, 1922.

1300 DODGE, Grenville M. *How We Built the Union Pacific Railway and Other Railway Papers and Addresses.* Washington, D.C., 1910.

1301 EGGERT, Gerald G. *Railroad Labor Disputes: The Beginnings of Federal Strike Policy.* Ann Arbor, 1967.

1302 ELLIS, D. M. "The Forfeiture of Railroad Land Grants, 1867-1894." *Miss Val Hist Rev,* XXXIII (1946), 27-60.

1303 FISH, Carl Russell. *The Restoration of Southern Railroads.* Madison, 1919.

1304 FOGEL, Robert W. *Railroads and American Economic Growth: Essays in Econometric History.* Baltimore, 1964.†

1305 FOGEL, Robert W. *The Union Pacific Railroad; a Case in Premature Enterprise.* Baltimore, 1960.

1306 GALLOWAY, John B. *First Transcontinental Railroad: Central Pacific, Union Pacific.* New York, 1950.

1307 GATES, Paul W. *The Illinois Central Railroad and Its Colonization Work.* Cambridge, Mass., 1934.

1308 GATES, Paul W. "The Railroad Land Grant Legend." *J Econ Hist,* XIV (1954), 143-146.

1309 GOODRICH, Carter. *Government Promotion of American Canals and Railroads: 1800-1900.* New York, 1960.

1310 GOODRICH, Carter. "Local Government Planning of Internal Improvements." *Pol Sci Q,* LXVI (1951), 411-445.

1311 GOODRICH, Carter, and Harvey H. SEGAL. "Baltimore's Aid to Railroads. A Study in the Municipal Planning of Internal Improvements." *J Econ Hist*, XIII (1953), 2-35.

1312 GORDON, Joseph H. *Illinois Railway Legislation and Commission Control since 1870.* Urbana, Ill, 1904.

1313 GREEN, Philip J. "Railroad Building from 1865 to 1885." *Univ N D Q J*, XIX (1928), 59-75.

1314 GREEVER, William S. "A Comparison of Railroad Land-Grant Policies." *Ag Hist*, XXV (1951), 83-90.

1315 GRODINSKY, Julius. *The Iowa Pool, a Study in Railroad Competition, 1870-1884.* Chicago, 1950.

1316 GRODINSKY, Julius. *Jay Gould, His Business Career, 1867-1892.* Philadelphia, 1957.

1317 GRODINSKY, Julius. *Transcontinental Railway Strategy, 1869-1893: A Study of Businessmen.* Philadelphia, 1962.

1318 HADLEY, Arthur T. *Railroad Transportation: Its History and Its Laws.* New York, 1885.

1319 HAMMOND, Matthew B. *Railway Rate Theories of the Interstate Commerce Commission.* Cambridge, Mass., 1911.

1320 HAMPTON, Taylor. *The Nickel Plate Road: The History of a Great Railroad.* Cleveland, 1947.

1321 HANEY, Lewis H. *A Congressional History of Railways in the United States.* Madison, 1910.

1322 HARBESON, Robert W. "Railroads and Regulation, 1877-1916: Conspiracy or Public Interest." *J Econ Hist*, XXVII (1967), 230-242.

1323 HEDGES, James B. "The Colonization Work of the Northern Pacific Railroad." *Miss Val Hist Rev*, XIII (1926), 311-342.

1324 HEDGES, James B. *Henry Villard and the Railways of the Northwest.* New Haven, 1930.

1325 HEDGES, James B. "Promotion of Immigration to the Pacific Northwest by the Railroads." *Miss Val Hist Rev*, XV (1928), 183-203.

1326 HENRY, Robert S. "The Railroad Land Grant Legend in American History Texts." *Miss Val Hist Rev*, XXXII (1945), 171-194, and "Comments on Henry's Article," *ibid.*, 557-576.

1327 HIRSHON, Stanley P. *Grenville M. Dodge: Soldier, Politician, Railroad Pioneer.* Bloomington, 1967.

1328 HUDSON, James F. *The Railways and the Republic.* New York, 1886.

1329 HUNT, Robert S. *Law and Locomotion: The Impact of the Railroad on Wisconsin Law in the Nineteenth Century.* Madison, 1958.

1330 HUSBAND, Joseph. *Story of the Pullman Car.* Chicago, 1917.

1331 *Industrial Commission Report*, Vol. IV (1900).

1332 JEANS, J. S. *Railway Problems.* London, 1887.

1333 JOHNSON, Emory R., and Thurman W. VAN METRE. *Principle of Railroad Transportation.* New York, 1921.

1334 KENNAN, George. *E. H. Harriman: A Biography.* Boston and New York, 1922.

1335 KIRKLAND, Edward C. *Men, Cities, and Transportation. A Study in New England History, 1820-1900.* 2 vols. Cambridge, Mass., 1948.

1336 KLEIN, Maury. "Southern Railroad Leaders, 1865-1893: Identities and Ideologies." *Bus Hist Rev,* XLII (1968), 288-310.

1337 KOLKO, Gabriel. *Railroads and Regulation, 1877-1916.* See 588.

1338 LANE, Wheaton J. *Commodore Vanderbilt: An Epic of the Steam Age.* New York, 1942.

1339 LANGSTROTH, Charles S., and Wilson STILZ. *Railway Cooperation: An Investigation of Railway Traffic Associations.* Philadelphia, 1899.

1340 LARRABEE, William. *Railroad Question: A Historical and Practical Treatise on Railroads, and Remedies for Their Abuses.* Chicago, 1893.

1341 LARSON, Henrietta M. *Jay Cooke: Private Banker.* Cambridge, Mass., 1936.

1342 LESLEY, Lewis B. "A Southern Transcontinental Railroad into California." *Pac Hist Rev,* V (1936), 52-60.

1343 LEWIS, Oscar. *The Big Four: The Story of Huntington, Stanford, Hopkins, and Crocker, and of the Building of the Central Pacific.* New York, 1938.

1344 MC ALLISTER, Samuel B. "Building the Texas and Pacific West of Fort Worth." *Yrbk W Tex Hist Assn,* IV (1928), 50-57.

1345 MC GUIRE, Peter S. "The Railroads of Georgia." *Ga Hist Q,* XVI (1932), 179-213.

1346 MERK, Frederick. "Eastern Antecedents of the Grangers." *Ag Hist,* XXIII (1949). See 604.

1347 MEYER, B. H. *Railway Legislation in the United States.* New York, 1903.

1348 MILLER, George H. "The Granger Laws: A Study of the Origins of State Railway Control in the Upper Mississippi Valley." Doctoral dissertation, University of Michigan, 1951.

1349 MILLER, George H. "Origins of the Iowa Granger Law." *Miss Val Hist Rev,* XL (1954), 657-680.

1350 MOODY, John. *The Railroad Builders; a Chronicle of the Welding of the States.* New Haven, 1921.

1351 NASH, Gerald D. "Origins of the Interstate Commerce Act of 1887." *Pa Hist,* XXIV (1957), 181-190.

1352 OVERTON, Richard C. *Burlington West: A Colonization History of the Burlington Railroad.* Cambridge, Mass., 1941.

1353 OVERTON, Richard C. *Gulf to Rockies: The Heritage of the Fort Worth and Denver Colorado and Southern Railways, 1861-1898.* Austin, 1953.

1354 PARKER, Edwin M. "The Southern Pacific Railroad and the Settlement of Southern California." *Pac Hist Rev,* VI (1937), 103-119.

1355 PARSONS, Frank. *The Railways, the Trusts, and the People.* Philadelphia, 1906.

1356 PEARSON, Henry G. *American Railroad Builder, John Murray Forbes.* Boston and New York, 1911.

1357 PERKINS, Jacob R. *Trails, Rails and War; the Life of General G. M. Dodge.* Indianapolis, 1929.

1358 PETERSON, Harold F. "Early Minnesota Railroads and the Quest for Settlers." *Minn Hist*, XIII (1932), 25-44.

1359 PETERSON, Harold F. "Some Colonization Projects of the Northern Pacific Railroad." *Minn Hist*, X (1929), 127-144.

1360 POOR, Henry V. *Manual of the Railroads of the United States.* Annually since 1868.

1361 PROUTY, Charles A. "National Regulation of Railroads." *Pub Am Econ Assoc*, 3d ser., IV (1903).

1362 PURCELL, Edward A. "Ideas and Interests: Businessmen and the Interstate Commerce Act." *J Am Hist*, LIV (1967), 561-578.

1363 PYLE, Joseph Gelpin. *Life of James J. Hill.* 2 vols. New York, 1951.

1364 RAE, John B. "Commissioner Sparks and the Railroad Land Grants." See 400.

1365 RIEGEL, Robert R. *The Story of the Western Railroads.* New York, 1926.†

1366 RIPLEY, William Z. *Railroads: Finance and Organization.* New York, 1915.

1367 RIPLEY, William Z. *Railroads: Rates and Regulations.* New York, 1912.

1368 SABIN, Edwin L. *Building the Pacific Railway.* Philadelphia and London, 1919.

1369 SABY, Rasmus S. *Railroad Legislation in Minnesota, 1849-1875.* St. Paul, 1915.

1370 SANBORN, John B. *Congressional Grants of Land in Aid of Railways.* Madison, 1899.

1371 SCHLEGEL, Marvin W. *Ruler of the Reading: The Life of Franklin B. Gowen 1836-1889.* Harrisburg, Pa., 1947.

1372 SHARFMAN, Isaiah L. *The Interstate Commerce Commission: A Study in Administrative Law and Procedure.* 5 vols. New York, 1931-1937.

1373 SMALLEY, Eugene V. *History of the Northern Pacific Railroad.* New York, 1883.

1374 SMALLEY, Harrison S. "Railway Rate Control in Its Legal Aspects." *Pub Am Econ Assn*, VII (1906), 327-473.

1375 STANWOOD, Edward. "Farmers and Railroads." *Old and New*, VIII (1873), 335-349.

1376 STARR, John W., Jr. *One Hundred Years of American Railroading.* New York, 1928.

1377 STERNE, Simon. *Railways in the United States. Their History, Their Relation to the State and an Analysis of the Legislation in Regard to Their Control.* New York, 1912.

1378 STEVENS, F. W. *The Beginnings of the New York Central Railroad: A History.* New York, 1926.

1379 STICKNEY, Alpheus B. *The Railway Problem.* St. Paul, 1891.

1380 STOVER, J. F. *American Railroads.* Chicago, 1961.†

1381 STOVER, J. F. *Railroads of the South, 1865-1900: A Study in Finance and Control.* Chapel Hill, 1955.

1382 TAYLOR, George R., and Irene D. NEU. *The American Railroad Network, 1861-1890.* Cambridge, Mass., 1956.

1383 THOMPSON, Slason. *A Short History of American Railroads.* New York, 1925.

1384 THRONE, Mildred. "The Repeal of the Iowa Granger Law, 1878." *Iowa J Hist,* LI (1953), 97-130.

1385 TROTTMAN, Nelson. *History of the Union Pacific: A Financial and Economic Survey.* New York, 1923.

1386 VAN OSS, Steven F. *American Railroads as Investments: A Handbook for Investors in American Railroad Securities.* New York, 1893.

1387 WARNER, A. G. "Railroad Problem in the West." *Pol Sci Q,* VI (1891), 66-89.

1388 WATERS, Lawrence, L. *Steel Rails to Santa Fe.* Lawrence, Kan., 1950.

1389 WELD, Louis D. H. *Private Freight Cars and American Railways.* New York, 1908.

1390 WHITE, Henry K. *History of the Union Pacific.* Chicago, 1895.

4. The Businessman

1391 AARON, Daniel. "Note on the Businessman and the Historian." *Ant Rev,* VI (1946), 575-584.

1392 ALLEN, Frederick L. *The Great Pierpont Morgan.* See 1138.

1393 APTHEKER, Herbert. *Laureates of Imperialism.* New York, 1954.

1394 BORNET, Vaughn D. "Those Robber Barons." *W Pol Q,* VI (1953), 342-346.

1395 BRIDGES, Hal. *Iron Millionaire: Life of Charlemagne Tower.* Philadelphia, 1952.

1396 BRIDGES, Hal. "The Robber Baron Concept in American History." *Bus Hist Rev,* XXXII (1958), 1-13.

1397 CARNEGIE, Andrew. *The Autobiography of Andrew Carnegie.* New York, 1920.

1398 CARNEGIE, Andrew. *The Empire of Business.* New York, 1902.

1399 CARNEGIE, Andrew. *Triumphant Democracy: Or Fifty Years' March of the Republic.* New York, 1886.

1400 CASSADY, Edward Everett. "The Business Man in the American Novel: 1856 to 1903." Doctoral dissertation, University of California, 1939.

1401 CLEWS, Henry. *Fifty Years in Wall Street*. See 1082.

1402 COCHRAN, Thomas C. "The Legend of the Robber Barons." *Pa Mag Hist Biog*, LXXIV (1950), 307-321.

1403 COCHRAN, Thomas C. *Railroad Leaders, 1845-1890: The Business Mind in Action*. Cambridge, Mass., 1953.

1404 CROFFUTT, W. A. *The Vanderbilts and the Story of Their Fortune*. Chicago, 1886.

1405 DE KRUIFF, Paul. *Seven Iron Men*. New York, 1929.

1406 DESTLER, Chester M. "Entrepreneurial Leadership among the Robber Barons: A Trial Balance." *J Econ Hist* (Suppl.), VI (1946), 28-49.

1407 DESTLER, Chester M. *Henry Demarest Lloyd*. See 123.

1408 DESTLER, Chester M. "The Opposition of American Businessmen to Social Control during the 'Gilded Age.'" *Miss Val Hist Rev*, XXXIX (1953), 641-672.

1409 DESTLER, Chester M. "'Wealth against Commonwealth,' 1894 and 1944." *Am Hist Rev*, L (1944), 49-69.

1410 DIAMOND, Sigmund. *The Reputation of the American Businessman*. Cambridge, Mass., 1955.

1411 EVANS, Henry O. *Iron Pioneer: Henry W. Oliver, 1840-1904*. New York, 1942.

1412 FLYNN, John T. *God's Gold*. New York, 1932.

1413 FULLER, Robert H. *Jubilee Jim; the Life of Colonel James Fisk*. New York, 1928.

1414 GIBBONS, H. A. *John Wanamaker*. 2 vols. New York, 1926.

1415 HACKER, Louis M. *The World of Andrew Carnegie, 1865-1901*. Philadelphia, 1967.

1416 HAYEK, F. S. von, ed. *Capitalism and the Historians*. Chicago, 1954.†

1417 HENDRICK, Burton J. *Life of Andrew Carnegie*. 2 vols. New York, 1932.

1418 HOLBROOK, Stewart. *The Age of the Moguls*. New York, 1953.†

1419 HOVEY, Carl. *The Life of J. P. Morgan*. London, 1912.

1420 HUGHES, Jonathan. *The Vital Few*. Boston, 1966.

1421 HUTCHINSON, William T. *Cyrus Hall McCormick*. 2 vols. New York, 1930.

1422 JOSEPHSON, Matthew. *Edison; a Biography*. New York, 1959.†

1423 JOSEPHSON, Matthew. *The Robber Barons*. New York, 1934.†

1424 KIRKLAND, Edward C., ed. *The Gospel of Wealth and Other Timely Essays by Andrew Carnegie*. Cambridge, Mass., 1962.†

1425 KIRKLAND, Edward C. "The Robber Barons Revisited." *Am Hist Rev*. LXVI (1960), 68-73.

1426 KLEIN, Maury. *The Great Richmond Terminal: A Study in Businessmen and Business Strategy.* Charlottesville, Va., 1970.

1427 KLEIN, Maury. "Southern Railroad Leaders, 1865-1893." See 1336.

1428 LEECH, Harper, and John C. CARROLL. *Armour and His Times.* New York and London, 1938.

1429 LLOYD, Henry Demarest. *Lords of Industry.* New York, 1916.

1430 LLOYD, Henry Demarest. *Wealth against Commonwealth.* New York, 1894.

1431 MILLER, William. "American Historians and the Business Elite." *J Econ Hist,* IX (1949), 184-208.

1432 MILLER, William. *Men in Business, Essays on the Historical Role of the Entrepreneur.* Cambridge, Mass., 1952.

1433 MILLER, William. "The Recruitment of the American Business Elite." *Q J Econ,* LXIV (1950), 242-253.

1434 MILLS, C. Wright. "The American Business Elite: A Collective Portrait." *J Econ Hist* (Suppl.), V (1945), 20-44.

1435 MOODY, John. *The Masters of Capital.* See 1163.

1436 MYERS, Gustavus. *History of Great American Fortunes.* Rev. ed. New York, 1936.

1437 NEVINS, Allan. *Study in Power: John D. Rockefeller, Industrialist and Philanthropist.* 2 vols. New York, 1953.

1438 NEVINS, Allan, and Matthew JOSEPHSON. "Should American History Be Rewritten?" *Sat Rev,* XXXVII (1954), 9-10, 44-46.

1439 REDLICH, Fritz. "The Business Leader as a 'Daimonic' Figure." *Amer J Econ Socio,* XII (1953 et seq.), 2 parts: pt. 1, 163-178; pt. 2, 289-299.

1440 REDLICH, Fritz. *History of American Business Leaders:* Vol. I: *Theory, Iron and Steel, Iron Ore Mining.* Ann Arbor, 1940.

1441 RISCHIN, Moses, ed. *The American Gospel of Success: Individualism and Beyond.* Chicago, 1965.†

1442 ROCKEFELLER, John D. *Random Reminiscences of Men and Events.* New York, 1909.

1443 SEARS, Marian V. "The American Businessman at the Turn of the Century." *Bus Hist Rev,* XXX (1956), 382-443.

1444 SOLGANICK, Allen. "The Robber Baron Concept and Its Revisionists." *Sci Soc,* XXIX (1965), 257-269.

1445 SUPPLE, Barry E. "A Business Elite: German-Jewish Financiers in Nineteenth Century New York." *Bus Hist Rev,* XXXI (1957), 143-178.

1446 TAUSSIG, F. W., and C. S. JOSLYN. *American Business Leaders: A Study in Social Origins and Social Stratification.* New York, 1932.

1447 TIPPLE, John. "The Anatomy of Prejudice: Origins of the Robber Baron Legend." *Bus Hist Rev,* XXXIII (1959), 510-523.

1448 WALL, Joseph Frazier. *Andrew Carnegie.* New York, 1970.

1449 WARNER, W. Lloyd, and J. ABEGGLEN. *Big Business Leaders in America.* New York, 1955.†

1450 WEISS, Richard. *The American Myth of Success: From Horatio Alger to Norman Vincent Peale.* New York, 1969.

1451 WHITE, Bouck. *Book of Daniel Drew: A Glimpse of the Fisk-Gould-Tweed Regime from the Inside.* Garden City, N.Y., 1910.

1452 WILLIAMSON, Harold F. *Edward Atkinson: The Biography of an American Liberal, 1827-1905.* Boston, 1934.

1453 WINKLER, John K. *Morgan the Magnificent.* Garden City, N.Y., 1930.

1454 WINKLER, John K. *Tobacco Tycoon: Story of James B. Duke.* New York, 1942.

1455 WOODRUFF, William. "History and the Businessmen." *Bus Hist Rev,* XXX (1956), 241-259.

1456 WYLLIE, Irvin G. *The Self-Made Man in America: The Myth of Rags to Riches.* New Brunswick, 1954.†

1457 WYLLIE, Irvin G. "Social Darwinism and the Businessman." *Proc Am Philos Soc,* CIII (1959), 629-635.

1458 YOUNGMAN, Anna P. *Economic Causes of Great Fortunes.* New York, 1909.

5. Distribution of Wealth and Income

1459 DOUGLAS, Paul H. *Real Wages in the United States, 1890-1926.* Boston, 1930.

1460 HEER, Clarence. *Income and Wages in the South.* Chapel Hill, 1930.

1461 HOLMES, George K. "The Concentration of Wealth." *Pol Sci Q,* VIII (1893), 589-600.

1462 KING, Wilford I. *The Wealth and Income of the People of the United States.* New York, 1915.

1463 KIRKLAND, Edward C. "Rhetoric and Rage over the Division of Wealth in the Eighteen Nineties." *Proc Am Ant Soc,* LXXIX (1969), 227-244.

1464 LONG, C. D. *Wages and Earnings in the United States, 1860-1890.* Princeton, 1960.

1465 MARTIN, Robert F. *National Income in the United States, 1799-1938.* New York, 1939.

1466 MULHALL, Michael G. "Power and Wealth of the United States." *N Amer Rev,* CLX (1895), 641-650.

1467 RATNER, Sidney. *New Light on the History of Great American Fortunes.* New York, 1953.†

1468 REES, Albert. *Real Wages in Manufacturing 1890-1914.* Princeton, 1961.

1469 SHEARMAN, Thomas. "The Owners of the United States." *Forum,* VIII (1889), 262-273.

1470 SPAHR, Charles B. *An Essay on the Present Distribution of Wealth in the United States.* New York, 1896.

1471 SUMNER, William Graham. "The Concentration of Wealth: Its Economic Justification." *Essays of William Graham Sumner.* New Haven, 1934.

1472 SUMNER, William Graham. *What Social Classes Owe to Each Other.* New York, 1883.†

1473 WATKINS, G. P. "The Growth of Large American Fortunes." *Pub Am Econ Assn,* 3d ser., VIII (1907), 735-904.

1474 WRIGHT, C. D. "Are the Rich Growing Richer?" *Atl Month,* LXXX (1897), 300-309.

XIV. America in the Gilded Age

1. The Rise of the City

1475 ADDAMS, Jane. *Twenty Years at Hull-House.* New York, 1910.†

1476 ATKINS, Gordon. *Health, Housing, and Poverty in New York City: 1865-1898.* New York, 1947.

1477 BALTZELL, E. Digby. *Philadelphia Gentlemen: The Making of a National Upper Class.* Glencoe, Ill., 1958.

1478 BEAN, Walton. *Boss Ruef's San Francisco.* See 769.†

1479 BEMIS, Edward Webster, ed. *Municipal Monopolies.* New York, 1899.

1480 BLAKE, Nelson M. *Water for the Cities: A History of Urban Water Supply Problems in the United States.* Syracuse, 1956.

1481 BRYCE, James. *The American Commonwealth.* See 57.†

1482 CASSEDY, James H. *Charles V. Chapin and the Public Health Movement.* Cambridge, Mass., 1962.

1483 CHAPIN, Charles V. *Municipal Sanitation in the United States.* Providence, 1901.

1484 COLE, Donald B. *Immigrant City: Lawrence, Massachusetts, 1845-1921.* Chapel Hill, 1963.

1485 CROOKS, James B. *Politics and Progress: The Rise of Urban Progressivism in Baltimore.* See 791.

1486 DAVIS, Allen F. *Spearhead for Reform: The Social Settlements and the Progressive Movement, 1890-1914.* See 796.†

1487 FOGELSON, Robert M. *The Fragmented Metropolis: Los Angeles, 1850-1930.* See 807.†

1488 GLAAB, Charles N., ed. *The American City: A Documentary History.* Homewood, Ill., 1963.†

1489 GLAAB, Charles N. "The History of the American City: A Bibliographical Survey." *The Study of Urbanization.* Eds. P. M. Hauser and L. F. Schnore. New York, 1965.

1490 GLAAB, Charles N. *Kansas City and the Railroads.* Madison, 1962.

1491 GLAAB, Charles N., and A. Theodore BROWN. *A History of Urban America.* New York, 1967.†

1492 GLAZIER, Willard. *Peculiarities of American Cities.* Philadelphia, 1883.

1493 GREEN, Constance M. *American Cities and the Growth of the Nation.* New York, 1957.

1494 GREEN, Constance M. *The Rise of Urban America.* New York, 1965.†

1495 GREEN, Constance M. *Washington: Capital City, 1879-1950.* Princeton, 1963.

1496 HAPGOOD, Hutchins. *The Spirit of the Ghetto.* New York, 1965.†

1497 HIRSCH, Werner Z., ed. *Urban Life and Form.* New York, 1963.†

1498 HOPKINS, Richard J. "Occupational and Geographic Mobility in Atlanta, 1870-1896." *J S Hist,* XXXIV (1968), 200-213.

1499 JACKSON, Joy J. *New Orleans in the Gilded Age, 1880-1896.* See 834.

1500 LOOMIS, Samuel Lane. *Modern Cities and Their Religious Problems.* New York, 1887.

1501 LUBOVE, Roy. *The Professional Altruist: The Emergence of Social Work as a Profession.* Cambridge, Mass., 1965.

1502 LUBOVE, Roy. *The Progressives and the Slums.* Pittsburgh, 1962.

1503 MC KELVEY, Blake. *The City in American History.* New York, 1969.

1504 MC KELVEY, Blake. *Rochester: The Flower City, 1855-1890.* Cambridge, Mass., 1949.

1505 MC KELVEY, Blake. *Rochester: The Quest for Quality, 1890-1925.* See 855.

1506 MC KELVEY, Blake. *The Urbanization of America.* New York, 1963.

1507 MAYER, Harold M., and Richard C. WADE. *Chicago: Growth of a Metropolis.* Chicago, 1969.

1508 MILLER, Zane L. *Boss Cox's Cincinnati.* See 864.†

1509 MORRIS, Lloyd R. *Incredible New York: High Life and Low Life of the Last Hundred Years.* New York, 1951.

1510 MUMFORD, Lewis. *The City in History.* New York, 1961.†

1511 MUMFORD, Lewis. *The Culture of Cities.* New York, 1938.†

1512 MUNRO, William Bennett. *The Government of American Cities.* New York, 1913.

1513 OSTERWEIS, Rollin G. *Three Centuries of New Haven, 1638-1938.* New Haven, 1953.

1514 PATTON, C. W. *The Battle for Municipal Reform: Mobilization and Attack, 1875-1900.* See 879.

1515 PIERCE, Bessie L. *The Rise of a Modern City* [*Chicago*], *1871-1893*. See 883.

1516 REPS, John William. *The Making of Urban America*. Princeton, 1965.

1517 REPS, John William. *Monumental Washington: The Planning and Development of the Capital Center*. Princeton, 1967.

1518 RIIS, Jacob. *The Battle with the Slum*. New York, 1902.

1519 RIIS, Jacob. *How the Other Half Lives*. New York, 1890.†

1520 ROBINSON, Charles M. *The Improvement of Towns and Cities*. New York, 1901.

1521 ROSE, William G. *Cleveland: The Making of a City*. Cleveland, 1950.

1522 SCHLESINGER, Arthur M. *The Rise of the City, 1877-1898*. New York, 1933.

1523 SCOTT, Mel. *American City Planning since 1890: A History Commemorating the Fiftieth Anniversary of the American Institute of Planners*. Berkeley and Los Angeles, 1969.

1524 SMITH, Duane A. *Rocky Mountain Mining Camps: The Urban Frontier*. Bloomington, 1967.

1525 STEFFENS, Lincoln. *The Shame of the Cities*. See 899.†

1526 STEFFENS, Lincoln. *The Struggle for Self-Government*. See 900.

1527 STEWART, Frank Mann. *A Half Century of Municipal Reform: The History of the National Municipal League*. Berkeley, 1950.

1528 STILL, Bayard. *Milwaukee: The History of a City*. Madison, 1948.

1529 STILL, Bayard, ed. *Mirror for Gotham: New York as Seen by Contemporaries from Dutch Days to the Present*. New York, 1956.

1530 SYRETT, Harold C. *The City of Brooklyn: 1865-1898*. New York, 1944.

1531 THERNSTROM, Stephan, and Richard SENNETT. *19th Century Cities: Essays in the New Urban History*. New Haven, 1969.†

1532 WALD, Lillian. *The House on Henry Street*. New York, 1915.†

1533 WARNER, Sam Bass, Jr. *Streetcar Suburbs: The Process of Growth in Boston, 1870-1900*. Cambridge, Mass., 1962.†

1534 WEBER, Adna F. *The Growth of Cities in the Nineteenth Century: A Study in Statistics*. New York, 1899.†

1535 WEBER, Max. *The City*. Trans. and ed. Don Martindale and Gertrude Neuwirth. Glencoe, Ill., 1958.†

1536 WHITE, A. T. *Better Homes for Working People*. New York, 1885.

1537 WOODRUFF, Clinton R. "The Progress of Municipal Reform in Philadelphia." *Har Week*, XXXVIII (1894), 1019.

2. Immigration

1538 ABBOTT, Edith. *Historical Aspects of the Immigration Problem.* Chicago, 1926.

1539 ABBOTT, Edith. *Immigration: Select Documents and Case Records.* Chicago, 1924.

1540 ABBOTT, Grace. *The Immigrant and the Community.* New York, 1917.

1541 ADAMIC, Louis. *From Many Lands.* New York, 1940.

1542 ANDER, O. Fritiof, ed. *In the Trek of the Immigrants: Essays Presented to Carl Wittke.* Rock Island, Ill., 1964.

1543 BABCOCK, Kendric C. *The Scandinavian Element in the United States.* Urbana, Ill., 1914.

1544 BARRY, Colman J. *The Catholic Church and German Americans.* Milwaukee, 1953.

1545 BERNARD, William S., ed. *American Immigration Policy: A Reappraisal.* New York, 1950.

1546 BERTHOFF, Roland T. *British Immigrants in Industrial America: 1790-1950.* Cambridge, Mass., 1953.

1547 BERTHOFF, Roland T. "Southern Attitudes toward Immigration, 1865-1914." *J S Hist,* XVII (1951), 328-360.

1548 BLEGEN, Theodore C. "The Competition of the Northwestern States for Immigrants." *Wis Mag Hist,* III (1919), 3-29.

1549 BLEGEN, Theodore C. "Minnesota's Campaign for Immigrants." *Yrbk Swed Hist Soc Am,* XI (1926), 3-28.

1550 BLEGEN, Theodore C. *Norwegian Migration to America.* Northfield, Minn., 1940.

1551 BOWERS, David F., ed. *Foreign Influences in American Life: Essays and Critical Bibliographies.* Princeton, 1944.†

1552 BROWN, Arthur J. "The Promotion of Emigration to Washington, 1854-1909." *Pac N W Q,* XXXVI (1945), 3-17.

1553 BROWN, Thomas N. *Irish-American Nationalism: 1870-1890.* Philadelphia, 1966.†

1554 BROWNE, Henry J. "The 'Italian Problem' in the Catholic Church of the United States, 1880-1900." *Hist Rec Stud (U S Cath Hist Soc),* XXXV (1946), 46-72.

1555 CAPEK, Thomas. *The Czechs in America.* Boston, 1920.

1556 COMMAGER, Henry S., ed. *Immigration and American History.* Minneapolis, 1961.

1557 COMMONS, John R. *Races and Immigrants in America.* New York, 1907.

1558 COOLIDGE, Mary R. *Chinese Immigration.* New York, 1909.

1559 CUNNINGHAM, George E. "The Italian, a Hindrance to White Solidarity in Louisiana, 1890-1898." *J Neg Hist,* L (1965), 22-36.

1560 CURTI, Merle, and Kendall BIRR. "The Immigrant and the American Image in Europe, 1860-1914." *Miss Val Hist Rev*, XXXVII (1950), 203-230.

1561 DAVIE, Maurice Rea. *World Immigration, with Special Reference to the United States*. New York, 1936.

1562 DAVIS, Jerome. *The Russian Immigrant*. New York, 1922.

1563 DE SANTIS, Vincent P. "The American Historian Looks at the Catholic Immigrant." *Roman Catholicism and the American Way of Life*. Ed. Thomas T. McAvoy. Notre Dame, 1960.

1564 ERICKSON, Charlotte. *American Industry and European Immigration: 1860-1885*. Cambridge, Mass., 1957.

1565 FAIRCHILD, Henry Pratt. *Greek Immigration to the United States*. New Haven, 1911.

1566 FAIRCHILD, Henry Pratt. "The Literacy Test and Its Making." *Q J Econ*, XXXI (1917), 447-460.

1567 FORESTER, Robert Franz. *The Italian Emigration of Our Times*. Cambridge, Mass., 1919.

1568 GIBSON, Florence E. *The Attitudes of the New York Irish toward State and National Affairs, 1848-1892*. See 812.

1569 HANDLIN, Oscar. *Race and Nationality in American Life*. Boston, 1957.†

1570 HANDLIN, Oscar. *The Uprooted: The Epic Story of the Great Migrations That Made the American People*. Boston, 1951.†

1571 HANDLIN, Oscar, ed. *Immigration as a Factor in American History*. Englewood Cliffs, N.J., 1959.†

1572 HANSEN, Marcus Lee. *The Immigrant in American History*. Cambridge, Mass., 1941.†

1573 HANSEN, Marcus Lee. "Official Encouragement of Immigration to Iowa." *Iowa J Hist*, XIX (1921), 159-196.

1574 HEALD, Morrell. "Business Attitudes toward European Immigration, 1880-1900." *J Econ Hist*, XIII (1953), 291-304.

1575 HIGHAM, John. "The American Party, 1886-1891." *Pac Hist Rev*, XIX (1950), 37-46.

1576 HIGHAM, John. *Strangers in the Land: Patterns of American Nativism, 1860-1925*. New Brunswick, 1955.†

1577 HOGLUND, A. William. *Finnish Immigrants in America, 1880-1920*. Madison, 1960.

1578 HOURWICH, Isaac A. *Immigration and Labor: The Economic Aspects of European Immigration to the United States*. New York, 1912.

1579 HUTHMACHER, J. Joseph. *A Nation of Newcomers*. New York, 1967.†

1580 ICHIHASHI, Yamato. *Japanese in the United States*. Stanford, 1932.

1581 JENKS, Jeremiah W., and W. Jenks LAUCK. *The Immigration Problem*. 5th ed. New York, 1921.

1582 JOHNSON, Stanley C. *A History of Immigration from the United Kingdom to North America, 1763-1912.* London, 1913.

1583 JONES, Maldwyn Allen. *American Immigration.* Chicago, 1960.†

1584 JOSEPH, Samuel. *Jewish Immigration to the United States from 1881 to 1910.* New York, 1914.

1585 KORMAN, Gerd. *Industrialization, Immigrant, and Americanizers: The View from Milwaukee, 1866-1921.* Madison, 1967.

1586 LEISERSON, William M. *Adjusting Immigrant and Industry.* New York, 1924.

1587 LOEWENBERG, Bert J. "Efforts of the South to Encourage Immigration, 1865-1900." *S Atl Q,* XXXIII (1934), 363-385.

1588 LORD, Eliot. *The Italians in America.* New York, 1905.

1589 LUEBKE, Frederick C. *Immigrants and Politics: The Germans of Nebraska, 1880-1900.* Lincoln, Neb., 1969.

1590 MILLER, Herbert A. *The School and the Immigrant.* Cleveland, 1916.

1591 MILLER, Stuart C. *The Unwelcome Immigrant: The American Image of the Chinese, 1785-1882.* Berkeley and Los Angeles, 1969.

1592 NELLI, Humbert S. *Italians in Chicago, 1880-1930. A Study in Ethnic Mobility.* New York, 1967.

1593 PARK, Robert E. *The Immigrant Press and Its Control.* New York and London, 1922.

1594 PARK, Robert E., and H. A. MILLER. *Old World Traits Transplanted.* New York, 1921.

1595 *Reports of the Immigration Commission.* 41 vols. Washington, D.C., 1911.

1596 RISCHIN, Moses. *The Promised City: New York Jews, 1870-1914.* Cambridge, Mass., 1962.†

1597 ROBERTS, Peter. *The New Immigration: A Study of the Industrial and Social Life of Southeastern Europeans in America.* New York, 1914.

1598 SALOUTOS, Theodore. *The Greeks in the United States.* Cambridge, Mass., 1964.

1599 SAVETH, Edward N. *American Historians and European Immigrants, 1875-1925.* New York, 1948.

1600 SCHELL, Herbert S. "Official Immigration Activities of Dakota Territory." *N D Hist Q,* VI (1932), 5-24.

1601 SMITH, Claude. "Official Efforts by the State of Mississippi to Encourage Immigration, 1868-1886." *J Miss Hist,* XXXII (1970), 327-340.

1602 SMITH, Timothy. "Immigrant Social Aspirations and American Education." *Am Q,* XXI (1969), 523-543.

1603 SMITH, William Carlson. *Americans in the Making: The Natural History of the Assimilation of Immigrants.* New York, 1939.

1604 SOLOMON, Barbara Miller. *Ancestors and Immigrants: A Changing New England Tradition.* Cambridge, Mass., 1956.

1605 STELLA, Antonio. *Some Aspects of Italian Immigration to the United States.* New York, 1924.

1606 STEPHENSON, George M. *A History of American Immigration, 1820-1924.* New York, 1926.

1607 SUTTLES, Gerald D. *The Social Order of the Slum.* Chicago, 1968.†

1608 THOMAS, William Isaac, and Florian ZNANIECKI. *The Polish Peasant in Europe and America.* 2 vols. New York, 1958.

1609 TYLER, Poyntz, ed. *Immigration and the United States.* New York, 1956.

1610 VANDERHILL, C. Warren. *Selling the Great Lake Frontier: Immigration to Michigan (1837-1924).* Lansing, 1970.

1611 WHYTE, William Foote. "Race Conflicts in the North End of Boston." *New Eng Q,* XII (1939), 623-642.

1612 WITTKE, Carl. *We Who Built America: The Saga of the Immigrant.* New York, 1939.

1613 YEARLEY, Clifford K. *Britons in American Labor: A History of United Kingdom Immigrants in American Labor, 1820-1914.* Baltimore, 1957.

3. Agriculture

1614 BAILEY, Joseph C. *Seaman A. Knapp, Schoolmaster of American Agriculture.* New York, 1945.

1615 BAILEY, Liberty Hyde, ed. *Cyclopedia of American Agriculture.* 3d ed. 4 vols. New York, 1910.

1616 BANKS, Enoch. *The Economics of Land Tenure in Georgia.* New York, 1905.

1617 BOGUE, Allan G. *From Prairie to Corn Belt: Farming on the Illinois and Iowa Prairies in the Nineteenth Century.* Chicago, 1963.†

1618 BOGUE, Allan G. *Money at Interest: The Farm Mortgage on the Middle Border.* Ithaca, N.Y., 1955.†

1619 BOGUE, Allan G., and Margaret B. BOGUE. " 'Profits' and the Frontier Land Speculator." *J Econ Hist,* XVII (1957), 1-24.

1620 BOGUE, Margaret B. *Patterns from the Sod: Land Use and Tenure in the Grand Prairie, 1850-1900.* Springfield, Ill., 1959.

1621 BRIGGS, Harold E. "Early Bonanza Farming in the Red River Valley of the North." *Ag Hist,* VI (1932), 26-37.

1622 BROOKS, Robert P. *The Agrarian Revolution in Georgia, 1865-1912.* See 471.

1623 CHASE, F. H. "Is Agriculture Declining in New England?" *N Eng Mag,* II (1890), 448-452.

1624 CLARK, Thomas D. *The Southern Country Editor.* Indianapolis, 1948.

1625 DICK, Everett N. *The Sod-House Frontier: 1854-1890.* New York, 1937.

1626 DRACHE, H. M. *The Day of the Bonanza: A History of Bonanza Farming in the Red River Valley of the North*. Fargo, N.D., 1964.

1627 EDWARDS, Everett E. "American Agriculture—The First 300 Years." *Yrbk Dept Ag*, Washington, D.C., 1940.

1628 EDWARDS, Everett E. "Middle Western Agricultural History as a Field of Research." *Miss Val Hist Rev*, XXIV (1937), 315-328.

1629 EFFERSON, John Norman. *The Production and Marketing of Rice*. New Orleans, 1952.

1630 FAIRCHILD, David G. *Exploring for Plants*. New York, 1930.

1631 FITE, Gilbert C. *The Farmer's Frontier, 1865-1900*. New York, 1966.†

1632 GATES, Paul W. *Fifty Million Acres: Conflicts over Kansas Land Policy, 1854-1890*. Ithaca, N.Y., 1954.†

1633 GRADY, Henry W. "Cotton and Its Kingdom." *Har Mag*, LXIII (1881), 719-734.

1634 HAMMOND, Matthew Brown. *The Cotton Industry—An Essay in American Economic History*. Ithaca, N.Y., 1897.

1635 HARDING, T. Swann. *Two Blades of Grass*. Norman, Okla., 1947.

1636 HAYTER, Earl W. *The Troubled Farmer, 1850-1900: Rural Adjustment to Industrialism*. DeKalb, Ill., 1968.

1637 HOWARD, Leland O. *Fighting the Insects*. New York, 1933.

1638 JESNESS, Oscar B., and William H. KERR. *Cooperative Purchasing and Marketing Organizations among Farmers in the United States*. Bull Dept Ag, No. 547. Washington, D.C., 1917.

1639 JOHNSTONE, P. H. "Old Ideas in Farm Life." *Farmers in a Changing World*. Washington, D.C., 1940.

1640 MC GINTY, G. W. "Changes in Louisiana Agriculture, 1860-1880." *La Hist Q*, XVIII (1935), 407-449.

1641 MALIN, James C. *Winter Wheat in the Golden Belt of Kansas*. Lawrence, Kan., 1944.

1642 MILLER, Glenn H., Jr. "The Hawkes Papers: A Case Study of a Kansas Mortgage Brokerage Business, 1871-1888." *Bus Hist Rev*, XXXII (1958), 293-310.

1643 MURRAY, Stanley N. "Railroads and the Agricultural Development of the Red River Valley of the North, 1870-1890." *Ag Hist*, XXXI (1957), 57-66.

1644 NOURSE, Edwin G. *American Agriculture and the European Market*. New York, 1924.

1645 ROBERT, Joseph H. *The Story of Tobacco in America*. New York, 1949.†

1646 ROGERS, William Warren. *Agrarianism in Alabama*. See 643.

1647 ROGIN, Leo. *The Introduction of Farm Machinery . . . during the Nineteenth Century*. Berkeley, 1931.

1648 SALOUTOS, Theodore. "The Agricultural Problem and Nineteenth-Century Industrialism." *Ag Hist*, XXII (1948), 156-174.

1649 SCHMIDT, Louis Bernard. "The Internal Grain Trade of the United States, 1860-1890." *Iowa J Hist Pol*, XIX (1921), 196-245, 414-445; XX (1922), 70-131.

1650 SHAFER, Joseph. *A History of Agriculture in Wisconsin*. Madison, 1922.

1651 SHANNON, Fred A. *The Farmers' Last Frontier: Agriculture, 1860-1897*. See 658.

1652 SHANNON, Fred A. "The Status of the Midwestern Farmer in 1900." *Miss Val Hist Rev*, XXXVII (1950), 491-510.

1653 SITTERSON, J. Carlyle. *Sugar Country: The Cane Sugar Industry in the South, 1753-1950*. Lexington, Ky., 1953.

1654 SMALLEY, E. V. "Isolation of Life on Prairie Farms." *Atl Month*, LXXII (1893), 375-382.

1655 SPELLMAN, William J., and Emanuel A. GOLDENWEISER. "Farm Tenantry in the United States." *Yrbk Dept Ag*. Washington, D.C., 1916.

1656 SWINGLE, F. B. "The Invention of the Twine Binder." *Wis Mag Hist*, X (1926), 35-41.

1657 TAYLOR, Carl C. *The Farmers' Movement, 1620-1920*. New York, 1953.

1658 TAYLOR, Henry C. *Outline of Agricultural Economics*. Rev. ed. New York, 1931.

1659 *The Final Report of the Industrial Commission*. Vol. X, 1901. Washington, D.C., 1902.

1660 THOMPSON, Carl W. *Costs and Sources of Farm-Mortgage Loans in the United States*. *Bull Dept Ag*, No. 384. Washington, D.C., 1916.

1661 TILLEY, Nannie May. *The Bright Tobacco Industry, 1860-1920*. Chapel Hill, 1948.

1662 TRUE, Alfred C. *A History of Agricultural Experimentation and Research in the United States, 1607-1925*. Department of Agriculture, Miscellaneous Publication No. 251. Washington, D.C., 1937.

1663 VANCE, Rupert B. *Human Geography of the South*. Chapel Hill, 1932.

1664 WALLER, J. L. "The Overland Movement of Cotton, 1866-1886." *S W Hist Q*, XXXV (1931), 137-145.

1665 WARREN, George Frederick. "Prices of Farm Products in the United States." *Bull Dept Ag*, No. 99. Washington, D.C., 1921.

1666 WHITE, Gerald T. "Economic Recovery and the Wheat Crop of 1897." *Ag Hist*, XIII (1939), 13-21.

1667 WILEY, Bell I. "Salient Changes in Southern Agriculture since the Civil War." *Ag Hist*, XIII (1939), 65-76.

1668 ZEICHNER, Oscar. "The Transition from Slave to Free Agricultural Labor in the Southern States." *Ag Hist*, XIII (1939), 22-32.

4. Labor

1669 ADAMIC, Louis. *Dynamite; the Story of Class Violence in America.* Rev. ed. New York, 1934.

1670 ADAMS, Thomas Sewall, and Helen L. SUMMER. *Labor Problems.* New York, 1905.

1671 AKIN, William C. "Arbitration and Labor Conflict: The Middle Class Panacea, 1886-1900." *Hist,* XXIX (1967), 565-583.

1672 ASHER, Robert. "Business and Workers' Welfare in the Progressive Era: Workmen's Compensation Reform in Massachusetts, 1880-1911." *Bus Hist Rev,* XLIII (1969), 452-475.

1673 AURAND, Harold W. "The Anthracite Strike of 1887-1888." *Pa Hist,* XXXV (1968), 169-185.

1674 BEDFORD, Henry F. *Socialism and the Workers in Massachusetts, 1886-1912.* Amherst, 1966.

1675 BERMAN, Edward. *Labor Disputes and the Presidents of the United States.* New York, 1924.

1676 BERRYMAN, Abraham, George T. STARNES, and Frank T. DEVYUER. *Labor in the Industrial South: A Survey of Wage and Living Conditions in the Major Industries at the New Industrial South.* Charlottesville, Va., 1930.

1677 BIMBA, Anthony. *The Molly Maguires.* New York, 1932.†

1678 BOGART, Ernest Ludlow, and Charles Manfred THOMPSON. *The Industrial State, 1870-1893.* Springfield, Ill., 1920.

1679 BONNETT, Clarence Elmore. *History of Employers' Associations in the United States.* New York, 1922.

1680 BRODY, David. *Steelworkers in America: The Nonunion Era.* Cambridge, Mass., 1960.†

1681 BROEHL, Wayne G., Jr. *The Molly Maguires.* Cambridge, Mass., 1964.†

1682 BROWNE, Henry J. *The Catholic Church and Knights of Labor.* Washington, D.C., 1949.

1683 BROWNE, Waldo Ralph. *Altgeld of Illinois.* See 103.

1684 BRUCE, R. V. *1877: Year of Violence.* See 325.†

1685 BUCHANAN, Joseph Ray. *The Story of the Labor Agitator.* New York, 1930.

1686 BUDER, Stanley. *Pullman: An Experiment in Industrial Order and Community Planning, 1880-1930.* Chicago, 1967.†

1687 BURKE, William Maxwell. *History and Function of Central Labor Unions.* New York, 1899.

1688 CAHILL, Marion Cotter. *Shorter Hours: A Study of the Movement since the Civil War.* New York and London, 1932.

1689 CARTER, Everett. "Haymarket Affair in Literature." *Am Q,* II (1950), 270-278.

1690 CHRISTIE, R. A. *Empire in Wood: A History of the Carpenters' Union.* Ithaca, N.Y., 1956.

1691 COLEMAN, James Walter. *The Molly Maguire Riots: Industrial Conflict in the Pennsylvania Coal Region.* Richmond, Va., 1936.

1692 COLEMAN, McAlister. *Men and Coal.* New York, 1943.

1693 COMMONS, John R., et al. *History of Labour in the United States.* 4 vols. New York, 1918-1935.

1694 COOMBS, Whitney. *The Wages of Unskilled Labor in Manufacturing Industries in the United States, 1890-1924.* New York, 1926.

1695 DACUS, J. A. *Annals of the Great Strikes in the United States.* Chicago and Philadelphia, 1877.

1696 DAVID, Henry. *The History of the Haymarket Affair.* New York, 1936.

1697 DEIBLER, Frederick S. *The Amalgamated Wood Workers' International Union of America; a Historical Study of Trade Unionism in Its Relation to the Development of an Industry.* Madison, 1912.

1698 DEWEES, Francis Percival. *The Molly Maguires. The Origin, Growth, and Character of the Organization.* Philadelphia, 1877.

1699 DOUGLAS, D. W. "Ira Steward on Consumption and Unemployment." *J Pol Econ,* XL (1932), 532-543.

1700 DUBOFSKY, Melvyn. "The Origin of Western Working Class Radicalism, 1890-1905." *Labor Hist,* VII (1966), 131-154.

1701 EGGERT, Gerald G. *Railroad Labor Disputes: The Beginnings of Federal Strike Policy.* See 1301.

1702 ELY, Richard T. *The Labor Movement in America.* Rev. ed. New York and London, 1905.

1703 ELY, Richard T. "Pullman." *Har Mag,* LXX (1885), 452-466.

1704 ENGBERG, George B. "The Knights of Labor in Minnesota." *Minn Hist,* XXII (1941), 367-390.

1705 EVANS, Chris. *History of United Mine Workers of America.* Indianapolis, 1918.

1706 FONER, Philip S. *History of the Labor Movement in the United States.* 4 vols. New York, 1947-1965.

1707 FORBES, Allyn B. "Literary Quest for Utopia 1880-1900." *Soc Forces,* VI (1927), 179-189.

1708 GALSTER, Augusta E. *The Labor Movement in Shoe Industry, with Special References to Philadelphia.* New York, 1924.

1709 GILMAN, Nicholas Paine. *Profit Sharing between Employer and Employee; a Study in the Evolution of the Wages System.* Boston and New York, 1889.

1710 GLÜCK, Elsie. *John Mitchell.* New York, 1929.

1711 GOLDMAN, Emma. *Living My Life.* Garden City, N.Y., 1931.

1712 GOMPERS, Samuel. *Seventy Years of Life and Labor.* 2 vols. New York, 1925.

1713 GREENE, Lorenzo J., and Carter G. WOODSON. *The Negro Wage Earner.* Washington, D.C., 1930.

1714 GROAT, George Gorham. *Attitude of Courts in Labor Cases; a Study in Social Legislation.* New York, 1911.

1715 GROB, Gerald N. "Reform Unionism: The National Labor Union." *J Econ Hist,* XIV (1954), 126-142.

1716 GROB, Gerald N. *Workers and Utopia: A Study of Ideological Conflict in the American Labor Movement, 1865-1900.* Evanston, Ill., 1961.†

1717 GUNTON, George. *Wealth and Progress.* New York, 1887.

1718 GUTMAN, Herbert G. "The Worker's Search for Power." *The Gilded Age: A Reappraisal.* Ed. H. Wayne Morgan. Syracuse, 1963.†

1719 HARRIS, Herbert. *American Labor.* New Haven, 1938.

1720 HARVEY, Rowland H. *Samuel Gompers, Champion of the Toiling Masses.* Stanford, 1935.

1721 JAMES, Alfred P. "First Convention of American Federation of Labor." *W Pa Hist Mag,* VI (1923), 201-233.

1722 JENSEN, Vernon H. *Heritage of Conflict.* Ithaca, N.Y., 1950.

1723 KIRK, William. *National Labor Federations in the United States.* Baltimore, 1906.

1724 KORMAN, Gerd. *Industrialization, Immigrants, and Americanization: The View from Milwaukee, 1866-1921.* See 1585.

1725 LAIDLER, Harry W. *Boycotts and the Labor Struggle.* New York, 1913.

1726 LASLETT, John. *Labor and Left: A Study of Socialist and Radical Influences in the American Labor Movement (1881-1924).* New York, 1970.

1727 LEIBY, James. *Carroll Wright and Labor Reform.* Cambridge, Mass., 1960.

1728 LESTER, Richard. *Economics of Labor.* New York, 1947.

1729 LEVASSEUR, E. *The American Workman.* Trans. T. S. Adams. Baltimore, 1900.

1730 LINDSEY, Almont. *The Pullman Strike.* See 374.†

1731 LORWIN, Lewis. *The American Federation of Labor.* Washington, D.C., 1933.

1732 LUM, Dyer Daniel. *Chicago Anarchists.* Chicago, 1886.

1733 MC MURRY, Donald L. *The Great Burlington Strike of 1888.* Cambridge, Mass., 1956.

1734 MC NEILL, G. E., ed. *The Labor Movement: The Problem of Today.* Boston, 1887.

1735 MANDEL, Bernard. *Samuel Gompers: A Biography.* Yellow Springs, Ohio, 1963.

1736 MANDEL, Bernard. "Samuel Gompers and the Negro Workers, 1886-1914." *J Neg Hist*, XL (1955), 34-60.

1737 MARSDEN, K. Gerald. "Patriotic Societies and American Labor: The American Protective Association in Wisconsin." *Wis Mag Hist*, XLI (1958), 287-294.

1738 MARSHALL, F. Ray. *Labor in the South*. Cambridge, Mass., 1967.

1739 MARTIN, Edward Winslow, and James Dabney MC CABE. *History of the Great Riots*. Philadelphia, 1877.

1740 MITCHELL, John. *Organized Labor*. Philadelphia, 1903.

1741 MITTLEMAN, Edward B. "Chicago Labor in Politics, 1877-1896." *J Pol Econ*, XXVIII (1920), 407-427.

1742 MONROE, Paul. "Profit Sharing in the United States." *Am J Socio*, I (1896), 685-709.

1743 ORTH, Samuel Peter. *Armies of Labor; a Chronicle of the Organized Wage-Earners*. New Haven, 1919.

1744 PARSONS, Albert R. *Anarchism: Its Philosophy and Scientific Basis as Defined by Some of Its Apostles*. Chicago, 1887.

1745 PELLING, Henry. *American Labor*. Chicago, 1960.†

1746 PERLMAN, Selig. *A History of Trade Unionism in the United States*. New York, 1922.

1747 PERLMAN, Selig. *A Theory of the Labor Movement*. New York, 1928.

1748 PETERSON, Florence. *Strikes in United States, 1880-1936*. Washington, D.C., 1938.

1749 PETERSON, James. "The Trade Unions and the Populist Party." *Sci Soc*, VIII (1944), 143-160.

1750 POWDERLY, Terrence V. *The Path I Trod*. New York, 1940.

1751 POWDERLY, Terrence V. *Thirty Years of Labor: 1859-1889*. Columbus, Ohio, 1889.

1752 RAYBACK, Joseph G. *A History of American Labor*. New York, 1959.†

1753 REED, Louis T. *The Labor Philosophy of Samuel Gompers*. New York, 1930.

1754 REES, Albert. *Real Wages in Manufacturing, 1890-1914*. See 1468.

1755 ROBBINS, Edwin Clyde. *Railway Conductors*. New York, 1914.

1756 ROBINSON, Jesse S. *Amalgamated Association of Iron, Steel, and Tin Workers*. Baltimore, 1920.

1757 ROWAN, Richard Wilmer. *Pinkerton's, a Detective Dynasty*. Boston, 1931.

1758 ROY, Andrew. *History of Coal Miners of the United States, from the Development of the Mines to the Close of the Anthracite Strike of 1902*. 3d ed. Columbus, Ohio, 1907.

1759 SAXTON, Alexander. "San Francisco Labor and the Populist and Progressive Insurgencies." *Pac Hist*, XXXIV (1965), 421-438.

1760 SCHOENHOF, Jacob. *Industrial Situation and the Question of Wages.* New York, 1885.

1761 SCHUSTER, Eunice M. *Native American Anarchism; a Study of Left-Wing American Individualism.* Northampton, Mass., 1932.

1762 SHANNON, Fred Albert. "Homestead Act and Labor Surplus." *Am Hist Rev,* XLI (1936), 637-651.

1763 SLANER, P. A. "Railroad Strikes of 1877." *Marx Q,* I (1937), 214-236.

1764 STIMSON, Frederick Jesup. *Handbook to Labor Law of the United States.* New York, 1896.

1765 STIMSON, Frederick Jesup. *Labor in Its Relations to Law.* New York, 1895.

1766 STOCKTON, F. T. *International Molders Union of North America.* Baltimore, 1921.

1767 SUFFERN, Arthur Elliott. *Coal Miners' Struggle for Industrial Status.* New York, 1926.

1768 SUFFERN, Arthur Elliott. *Conciliation and Arbitration in Coal Industry of America.* Boston, 1915.

1769 TAFT, Philip. *The AFL in the Time of Gompers.* New York, 1957.

1770 TAFT, Philip. *Organized Labor in American History.* New York, 1964.

1771 THERNSTROM, Stephan. *Poverty and Progress: Social Mobility in a Nineteenth-Century City.* Cambridge, Mass., 1964.†

1772 TODES, Charlotte. *William H. Sylvis and the National Labor Union.* New York, 1942.

1773 TRUMBULL, Lyman. *The Cause and Suggestion of the Cure of Labor Troubles.* Chicago, 1894.

1774 ULMAN, Lloyd. *The Rise of the National Trade Union.* Cambridge, Mass., 1955.

1775 WARE, Norman J. *The Labor Movement in the United States, 1860-1895.* New York, 1929.†

1776 WESLEY, Charles H. *Negro Labor in the United States.* New York, 1927.

1777 WISH, Harvey. "Governor Altgeld Pardons Anarchists." *Ill State Hist Soc J,* XXXI (1938), 424-448.

1778 WITTE, Edwin. *Government in Labor Disputes.* New York, 1932.

1779 WOLMAN, Leo. *The Boycott in American Trade Unions.* Baltimore, 1916.

1780 WOLMAN, Leo. *The Growth of American Trade Unions.* New York, 1924.

1781 WOLFF, Leon. *Lockout: The Story of the Homestead Strike of 1892.* See 439.

1782 WRIGHT, Carroll Davidson. *Industrial Conciliation and Arbitration.* Boston, 1881.

1783 YELLOWITZ, Irvin. *The Position of the Worker in American Society, 1865-1896.* Englewood Cliffs, N.J., 1969.†

1784 ZEISLER, Sigmund. "Reminiscences of the Anarchist Case." *Ill Law Rev*, XXI (1927), 224-250.

5. Religion

1785 ABELL, Aaron. *American Catholicism and Social Action*. Garden City, N.Y., 1960.†

1786 ABELL, Aaron. "Reception of Leo XIII's Labor Encyclical." *Rev Pol*, VII (1945), 464-495.

1787 ABELL, Aaron. *The Urban Impact on American Protestantism, 1865-1900*. Cambridge, Mass., 1943.

1788 ADAMS, O. F. "Aristocratic Drift of Protestantism." *N Am Rev*, CXLII (1886), 194-199.

1789 ADDISON, James Thayer. *The Episcopal Church in the United States, 1789-1931*. New York, 1951.

1790 ANDERSON, Hugh George. *Lutheranism in the Southeastern States, 1860-1886: A Social History*. The Hague, 1969.

1791 ARMSTRONG, Maurice W., et al., eds. *The Presbyterian Enterprise: Sources of American Presbyterian History*. Philadelphia, 1956.

1792 ATKINS, Gaius Glenn, and Frederick Louis FAGLEY. *History of American Congregationalism*. Boston and Chicago, 1942.

1793 BARRY, Colman J. *The Catholic Church and German Americans*. See 1544.

1794 BATES, Ernest S., and John V. DITTEMORE. *Mary Baker Eddy*. New York, 1932.

1795 BEASLEY, Norman. *The Cross and the Crown: The History of Christian Science*. New York, 1952.

1796 BEETS, Henry. *The Christian Reformed Church in North America*. Grand Rapids, Mich., 1923.

1797 BODEIN, V. P. *The Social Gospel of Walter Rauschenbusch and Its Relation to Religious Education*. New Haven, 1944.

1798 BOLLER, Paul F. *American Thought in Transition: The Impact of Evolutionary Naturalism, 1865-1900*. Chicago, 1969.†

1799 BOSHER, Robert S., comp. "The Episcopal Church and American Christianity: A Bibliography." *Hist Mag*, XIX (1950), 369-384.

1800 BRADFORD, Gamaliel. *D. L. Moody, A Worker in Souls*. New York, 1927.

1801 BRAUER, Jerald C. *Protestantism in America*. Rev. ed. Philadelphia, 1966.

1802 BROWN, Ira V. *Lyman Abbot, Christian Evolutionist*. Cambridge, Mass., 1953.

1803 BROWNE, Henry J. *The Catholic Church and Knights of Labor*. See 1682.

1804 BUCKLEY, James M. *A History of Methodists in the United States*. New York, 1903.

1805 CLARK, Elmer Talmage. *The Small Sects in America*. Rev. ed. New York, 1949.†

1806 COMMONS, John R. *Social Reform and the Church*. New York, 1894.

1807 CROSS, Robert D. *The Emergence of Liberal Catholicism in America*. Cambridge, Mass., 1958.†

1808 CROSS, Robert D., ed. *The Church and the City, 1865-1910*. Indianapolis, 1967.†

1809 CUNNINGHAM, Raymond J. "The Impact of Christian Science on the American Churches, 1880-1910." *Am Hist Rev*, LXXII (1967), 885-905.

1810 DAKIN, Edwin F. *Mrs. Eddy: The Biography of a Virginal Mind*. New York, 1930.†

1811 DE GROOT, Thomas Alfred, and Winfred E. GARRISON. *The Disciples of Christ, a History*. St. Louis, 1948.

1812 DESMOND, Humphrey Joseph. *The APA Movement, a Sketch*. Washington, D.C., 1912.

1813 DOMBROWSKI, James. *The Early Days of Christian Socialism in America*. New York, 1936.

1814 DORN, Jacob H. *Washington Gladden: Prophet of the Social Gospel*. Columbus, Ohio, 1967.

1815 EATON, Clement. "Professor James Woodrow and the Freedom of Teaching in the South." *J S Hist*, XXVIII (1962), 3-17.

1816 EDDY, Mary Baker. *Retrospections*. Boston, 1891.†

1817 ELLIS, John Tracy. *American Catholicism*. Chicago, 1956.†

1818 ELLIS, John Tracy. "Church and State: An American Catholic Tradition." *Har Mag*, CCVII (1953), 63-67.

1819 ELLIS, John Tracy. *The Life of James Cardinal Gibbons*. 2 vols. Milwaukee, 1952.

1820 ELY, Richard T. *Social Aspects of Christianity*. New York, 1889.

1821 FINDLAY, James F., Jr. *Dwight L. Moody: American Evangelist, 1837-1899*. Chicago, 1969.

1822 GAUSTAD, Edwin Scott. *A Religious History of America*. New York, 1967.

1823 GLADDEN, Washington. *Applied Christianity*. Boston and New York, 1886.

1824 GLADDEN, Washington. *Recollections*. See 258.

1825 GLAZER, Nathan. *American Judaism*. Chicago, 1957.†

1826 HARDON, John A. *The Protestant Churches of America*. Westminster, Md., 1956.†

1827 HIBBEN, Paxton. *Henry Ward Beecher, an American Portrait*. New York, 1927.

1828 HIGHAM, John. "Anti-Semitism in the Gilded Age: A Reinterpretation." *Miss Val Hist Rev*, XLIII (1957), 559-578.

1829 HIGHAM, John. *Strangers in the Land: Patterns of American Nativism.* See 1576.†

1830 HOPKINS, Charles Howard. *History of the Y. M. C. A. in North America.* New York, 1951.

1831 HOPKINS, Charles Howard. *The Rise of the Social Gospel in American Protestantism, 1865-1915.* New Haven, 1940.

1832 HUDSON, Winthrop S. *American Protestantism.* Chicago, 1961.†

1833 IRELAND, John. *The Church and Modern Society, Lectures and Addresses.* 2d ed. Chicago and New York, 1897.

1834 JOHNSON, R. H. "Baptists in the Age of Big Business." *J Rel,* XI (1931), 63-85.

1835 KALASSAY, Louis A. "The Educational and Religious History of the Hungarian Reformed Church in the United States." Doctoral dissertation, University of Pittsburgh, 1940.

1836 KLEIN, Harry Martin John. *The History of the Eastern Synod of the Reformed Church in the United States.* Lancaster, Pa., 1943.

1837 LEVINGER, Lee Joseph. *A History of the Jews in the United States.* Rev. ed. Cincinnati, 1949.

1838 LINN, William A. *The Story of the Mormons from the Date of Their Origins to the Year 1901.* New York, 1902.

1839 LOEWENBERG, B. J. "Controversy over Evolution in New England." *N Eng Q,* VIII (1935), 232-257.

1840 MC AVOY, Thomas T. "Americanism, Fact and Fiction." *Am Cath Hist Rev,* XXXI (1945), 133-153.

1841 MC AVOY, Thomas T. *The Great Crises in American Catholic Church History.* Chicago, 1957.

1842 MC AVOY, Thomas T. *A History of the Catholic Church in the United States.* Notre Dame, 1969.

1843 MAC DONALD, George E. H. *Fifty Years of Free Thought.* 2 vols. New York, 1929-1931.

1844 MC LOUGHLIN, William. *Modern Revivalism: Charles Grandison Finney to Billy Graham.* New York, 1959.

1845 MARTIN, Walter R. *The Rise of the Cults.* Grand Rapids, Mich., 1955.

1846 MATHESON, Richard R. *Faiths, Cults, and Sects of America from Atheism to Zen.* Indianapolis and New York, 1960.

1847 MAY, Henry F. *Protestant Churches and Industrial America.* New York, 1949.†

1848 MAYNARD, Theodore. *The Story of American Catholicism.* New York, 1943.

1849 MORSE, C. M. "Church and Working Man." *Forum,* VI (1888), 653-661.

1850 MOYNIHAN, James H. *The Life of Archbishop John Ireland.* New York, 1953.

1851 MULDER, William, and A. Russell MORTENSEN, eds. *Among the Mormons.* New York, 1957.

1852 OLMSTEAD, Clifton E. *History of Religion in the United States.* Englewood Cliffs, N.J., 1960.†

1853 PEEL, Robert. *Christian Science: Its Encounter with American Culture.* New York, 1958.

1854 PERRY, H. F. "The Workingman's Alienation from the Church." *Am J Sociol,* IV (1899), 622-629.

1855 PERRY, William Stevens. *The History of the American Episcopal Church, 1587-1883.* 2 vols. Boston, 1885.

1856 PERSONS, Stow. *Free Religion: An American Faith.* New Haven, 1947.

1857 PHILIPSON, David. *The Reform Movement in Judaism.* Rev. ed. New York, 1931.

1858 RAUSCHENBUSCH, Walter. *Christianity and the Social Crisis.* New York, 1907.†

1859 SANDEEN, Ernest R. *The Roots of Fundamentalism: British and American Millenarianism.* Chicago, 1970.†

1860 SHARPE, D. R. *Rauschenbusch.* New York, 1942.

1861 SMITH, James W., and A. Leland JAMISON, eds. *Religion in American Life.* 4 vols. Princeton, 1961.

1862 SPERRY, Willard L. *Religion in America.* Cambridge, Mass., 1946.

1863 STRONG, Josiah. *The New Era.* New York, 1893.

1864 SWEET, William Warren. *The Story of Religion in America.* Rev. ed. New York, 1950.

1865 TANIS, Edward J. *What the Sects Teach; Jehovah's Witnesses, Seventh Day Adventists, Christian Science [and] Spiritism.* Grand Rapids, Mich., 1958.

1866 THOMAS, Allen Clapp. *A History of the Friends in America.* Philadelphia, 1930.

1867 TORBET, Robert G. *A History of the Baptists.* Philadelphia, 1950.†

1868 WANGLER, Thomas E. "John Ireland and the Origins of Liberal Catholicism in the United States." *Am Cath Hist Rev,* LVI (1971), 617-629.

1869 WARREN, Sidney. *American Free Thought, 1860-1914.* New York, 1943.

1870 WEISBERGER, Bernard A. *They Gathered at the River.* Boston, 1958.†

1871 WHITE, Edward A. *Science and Religion in American Thought: The Impact of Naturalism.* Stanford, 1952.

1872 WILBUR, Sybil. *The Life of Mary Baker Eddy.* Boston, 1938.

1873 WISBEY, Herbert A., Jr. *Soldiers without Swords: A History of the Salvation Army in the United States.* New York, 1955.

1874 ZENOS, Andrew C. *Presbyterianism in America: Past, Present, and Prospective.* New York, 1937.

6. The Negro

1875 ABRAMOWITZ, Jack. "The Negro in the Agrarian Revolt." See 442.

1876 ABRAMOWITZ, Jack. "The Negro in the Populist Movement." See 443.

1877 ALLPORT, Gordon W. *The Nature of Prejudice.* Cambridge, Mass., 1954.†

1878 BACOTE, Clarence A. "Negro Proscriptions, Protests, and Proposed Solutions in Georgia, 1880-1908." *J S Hist,* XXV (1959), 471-498.

1879 BACOTE, Clarence A. "Some Aspects of Negro Life in Georgia, 1880-1908." *J Neg Hist,* XLIII (1958), 186-213.

1880 BARDOLPH, Richard. *The Civil Rights Record: Black Americans and the Law.* New York, 1970.†

1881 BLAIR, Lewis. *A Southern Prophecy: The Prosperity of the South Dependent upon the Elevation of the Negro.* Ed. C. Vann Woodward. Boston, 1964.

1882 BLOCH, Herman D. "The New York City Negro and Occupational Eviction, 1869-1910." *Int Rev Soc Hist,* V (1960), 26-38.

1883 BRAWLEY, Benjamin G. *A Social History of the American Negro.* New York, 1921.

1884 BYRANT, Lawrence C., ed. *Negro Lawmakers in the South Carolina Legislature, 1868-1902.* Orangeburg, S.C., 1968.

1885 BUCK, Paul H. *The Road to Reunion: 1865-1900.* See 58.†

1886 CABLE, George Washington. *The Negro Question: A Selection of Writings on Civil Rights in the South.* Ed. Arlin Turner. New York, 1890.†

1887 CALCOTT, Margaret Law. *The Negro in Maryland Politics, 1870-1912.* Baltimore, 1969.

1888 CHAFE, William H. "The Negro and Populism." See 486.

1889 CHEEK, William F. "A Negro Runs for Congress: John Mercer Langston and the Virginia Campaign of 1888." *J Neg Hist,* LII (1967), 14-34.

1890 CHESNUTT, Charles Waddell. *The Marrow of Tradition.* Boston, 1901.†

1891 CLANCY, John J., Jr. "A Mugwump [E. L. Godkin] on Minorities." *J Neg Hist,* L (1966), 174-193.

1892 CROFTS, Daniel W. "The Black Response to the Blair Education Bill." *J S Hist,* XXXVII (1971), 41-65.

1893 CROWE, Charles. "Tom Watson, Populists, and Blacks Reconsidered." See 499.

1894 DANIEL, W. Harrison. "Virginia Baptists and the Negro, 1865-1902." *Va Mag Hist Biog,* LXXVI (1968), 340-363.

1895 DE SANTIS, Vincent P. "Negro Dissatisfaction with Republican Policy in the South, 1882-1884." *J Neg Hist,* XXXVI (1951), 148-159.

1896 DE SANTIS, Vincent P. "The Republican Party and the Southern Negro, 1877-1897." *J Neg Hist,* XLV (1960), 71-87.

1897 DE SANTIS, Vincent P. *Republicans Face the Southern Question.* See 63.

1898 DETHLOFF, Henry C., and Robert R. JONES. "Race Relations in Louisiana, 1877-98." *La Hist,* IX (1968), 301-323.

1899 DIXON, Thomas. *The Leopard's Spots, a Romance of the White Man's Burden, 1865-1900.* New York, 1903.

1900 DOYLE, Bertram W. *The Etiquette of Race Relations in the South.* Chicago, 1937.

1901 DU BOIS, W. E. B. "The Conditions of Negroes in Various Cities." *Bull Dept Labor* (May 1897), 257-369.

1902 DU BOIS, W. E. B. *Dusk of Dawn.* New York, 1940.†

1903 DU BOIS, W. E. B. *The Philadelphia Negro.* Philadelphia, 1899.†

1904 DU BOIS, W. E. B. *The Souls of Black Folk: Essays and Sketches.* Ed. Saunders Redding. Greenwich, Conn., 1961.†

1905 DURHAM, Philip, and Everett L. JONES. *Negro Cowboys.* New York, 1965.

1906 EDMONDS, Helen. *The Negro and Fusion Politics in North Carolina.* Chapel Hill, 1951.

1907 FISHEL, Leslie H., Jr. "The Negro in Northern Politics, 1870-1900." *Miss Val Hist Rev,* XLII (1955), 466-489.

1908 FISHEL, Leslie H., Jr. "The North and the Negro, 1865-1900: A Study in Race Discrimination." Doctoral dissertation, Harvard University, 1954.

1909 FISHEL, Leslie H., Jr. "Repercussions of Reconstruction: The Northern Negro, 1870-1883." *Civil War Hist,* XIV (1968), 325-345.

1910 FLYNN, John P. "Booker T. Washington: Uncle Tom or Wooden Horse." *J Neg Hist,* LIV (1969), 262-274.

1911 FORTUNE, T. Thomas. *Black and White: Land, Labor, and Politics in the South.* New York, 1884.

1912 FRANKLIN, John Hope. *From Slavery to Freedom: A History of American Negroes.* 3d ed. New York, 1967.†

1913 FRANKLIN, John Hope. "Jim Crow Goes to School." *S Atl Q,* LVIII (1959), 225-235.

1914 FRAZIER, E. Franklin. *The Negro in the United States.* Rev. ed. New York, 1957.†

1915 GATEWOOD, Willard B. "William D. Crum: A Negro in Politics." *J Neg Hist,* LIII (1968), 301-320.

1916 GNATZ, William. "The Negro and the Populist Movement in the South." See 545.

1917 GREENE, Lorenzo J., and Carter G. WOODSON. *The Negro Wage Earner.* See 1713.

1918 GUTMAN, Herbert G. "Peter H. Clark: Pioneer Negro Socialist." *J Neg Educ,* XXXIV (1965), 413-418.

1919 HALLER, John S. "The Physician versus the Negro: Medical and Anthropological Concepts of Race in the Late Nineteenth Century." *Bull Hist Med,* XLIV (1970), 154-167.

1920 HAMILTON, Samuel. "New Race Question in the South." *Arena*, XXVII (1902), 352-358.

1921 HARLAN, Louis R. "Booker T. Washington and the White Man's Burden." *Am Hist Rev*, LXXI (1966), 441-467.

1922 HARLAN, Louis R. "Booker T. Washington in Biographical Perspective." *Am Hist Rev*, LXXV (1970), 1581-1599.

1923 HARLAN, Louis R. "The Southern Education Board and the Race Issue in Public Education." *J S Hist*, XXIII (1957), 189-202.

1924 HIRSHON, Stanley P. *Farewell to the Bloody Shirt*. See 73.

1925 JARRELL, Hampton. *Wade Hampton and the Negro, the Road Not Taken*. Charleston, S.C., 1949.

1926 JOHNSON, Charles S. *The Negro in American Civilization*. New York, 1930.

1927 JOHNSON, Charles S. *Patterns of Negro Segregation*. New York, 1943.†

1928 JOHNSON, Franklin. *The Development of State Legislation Concerning the Free Negro*. New York, 1919.

1929 JOHNSON, Guion Griffis. "The Ideology of White Supremacy, 1876-1910." *Essays in Southern History Presented to Joseph Gregoire de Roulhac Hamilton. . . .* Ed. Fletcher M. Green. Chapel Hill, 1949.

1930 KESSLER, Sidney H. "The Organization of Negroes in the Knights of Labor." *J Neg Hist*, XXVII (1952), 248-276.

1931 LEWINSON, Paul. *Race, Class, and Party: A History of Negro Suffrage and White Politics in the South*. New York, 1932.

1932 LEWIS, Elsie. "The Political Mind of the Negro, 1865-1900." *J S Hist*, XXI (1955), 189-202.

1933 LOGAN, Frenise A. "The Economic Status of the Town Negro in Post-Reconstruction North Carolina." *N C Hist Rev*, XXXV (1958), 448-460.

1934 LOGAN, Frenise A. *The Negro in North Carolina, 1876-1894*. Chapel Hill, 1964.

1935 LOGAN, Rayford W. *The Betrayal of the Negro from Rutherford B. Hayes to Woodrow Wilson*. New York, 1965.†

1936 LOGAN Rayford W. *The Negro in the United States*. New York, 1957.†

1937 LYNCH, John R. *Reminiscences of an Active Life*. See 277.

1938 MABRY, William A. "Disfranchisement of the Negro in Mississippi." *J S Hist*, IV (1938), 318-333.

1939 MC DONOUGH, John. "Manuscript Resources for the Study of Negro Life and History." *Q J Lib Cong*, XXVI (1969), 126-148.

1940 MC PHERSON, James M. "White Liberals and Black Power in Negro Education, 1865-1915." *Am Hist Rev*, LXXV (1970), 1357-1386.

1941 MANDEL, Bernard. "Samuel Gompers and the Negro Workers, 1886-1914." See 1736.

1942 MANGUM, Charles S., Jr. *The Legal Status of the Negro*. Chapel Hill, 1940.

1943 MATHEWS, John M. *Legislative and Judicial History of the Fifteenth Amendment*. Baltimore, 1909.

1944 MECKLIN, John M. *Democracy and Race Friction*. New York, 1914.

1945 MEIER, August. "Booker T. Washington and the Negro Press." *J Neg Hist*, XXXVIII (1953), 67-90.

1946 MEIER, August. *Negro Thought in America, 1880-1915; Racial Ideologies in the Age of Booker T. Washington*. Ann Arbor, 1963.†

1947 MEIER, August. "Toward a Reinterpretation of Booker T. Washington." *J S Hist*, XXIII (1957), 220-227.

1948 MEIER, August, and Elliott M. RUDWICK. *From Plantation to Ghetto: An Interpretive History of American Negroes*. New York, 1966.†

1949 MILLER, Elizabeth W. *The Negro in America: A Bibliography*. See 26.†

1950 MURRAY, Pauli. *State Laws on Race and Color*. Cincinnati, 1951.

1951 MYRDAL, Gunnar. *An American Dilemma: The Negro Problem and Modern Democracy*. 2 vols. New York, 1944.†

1952 PETTIGREW, Thomas F. *A Profile of the American Negro*. Princeton, 1964.†

1953 PORTER, Kenneth W. "Negro Labor in the Western Cattle Industry, 1866-1900." *Labor Hist*, X (1969), 346-374.

1954 PUTNAM, Carleton. *Race and Reason: A Yankee View*. Washington, D.C., 1961.

1955 QUARLES, Benjamin. *Frederick Douglass*. Washington, D.C., 1948.†

1956 RAPER, Arthur F. *The Tragedy of Lynching*. Chapel Hill, 1933.†

1957 REDKEY, Edwin S. *Black Exodus: Black Nationalism and Back-to-Africa Movements, 1890-1910*. New Haven and London, 1969.†

1958 REIMERS, David M., ed. *The Black Man in America since Reconstruction*. New York, 1970.†

1959 RICE, Lawrence D. *The Negro in Texas, 1874-1900*. Baton Rouge, 1971.

1960 RODABAUGH, James H. "The Negro in Ohio." *J Neg Hist*, XXXI (1946), 9-29.

1961 ROSS, Frank A., and Louise V. KENNEDY. *A Bibliography of Negro Migration*. New York, 1934.

1962 RUBIN, Louis D., Jr. *George W. Cable: The Life and Times of a Southern Heretic*. New York, 1969.

1963 RUBIN, Louis D., Jr. *Teach the Freedman: The Correspondence of Rutherford B. Hayes and the Slater Fund for Negro Education, 1881-1892*. 2 vols. Baton Rouge, 1959.

1964 SAUNDERS, Robert. "Southern Populists and the Negro, 1892-1905." See 651.

1965 SAVAGE, W. S. "The Negro on the Mining Frontier." *J Neg Hist,* XXVIII (1943), 9-29.

1966 SCHEINER, Seth M. *Negro Mecca: A History of the Negro in New York City, 1865-1920.* New York, 1965.†

1967 SHAPIRO, Herbert. "The Populists and the Negro: A Reconsideration." *Making of Black America.* Eds. August Meier and Elliott Rudwick. New York, 1969.

1968 SIMKINS, Francis B. "Ben Tillman's View of the Negro." See 662.

1969 SINKLER, George. "Benjamin Harrison and the Matter of Race." See 412.

1970 SINKLER, George. "Race: Principles and Policies of Rutherford B. Hayes." See 413.

1971 SINKLER, George. *The Racial Attitudes of American Presidents from Abraham Lincoln to Theodore Roosevelt.* Garden City, N.Y., 1971.

1972 SMITH, Samuel D. *The Negro in Congress, 1870-1901.* Chapel Hill, 1940.

1973 SMITH, Willard H. "William Jennings Bryan and Racism." *J Neg Hist,* LIV (1969), 127-149.

1974 SPEAR, Allan H. *Black Chicago: The Making of a Negro Ghetto.* Chicago, 1967.†

1975 SPENCER, Samuel R., Jr. *Booker T. Washington and the Negro's Place in American Life.* Boston, 1955.†

1976 SPERO, Sterling D., and Abram L. HARRIS. *The Black Worker.* New York, 1931.†

1977 STEPHENSON, Gilbert T. *Race Distinctions in American Law.* New York, 1910.

1978 STONE, Alfred Holt. *Studies in the American Race Problem.* New York, 1908.

1979 TAYLOR, Alrutheus A. *The Negro in Tennessee, 1865-1880.* Washington, D.C., 1941.

1980 TEBEAU, C. W. "Some Aspects of Planter-Freedman Relations." *J Neg Hist,* XXI (1936), 130-150.

1981 THORNBROUGH, Emma Lou. "American Negro Newspapers, 1880-1914." *Bus Hist Rev,* XL (1966), 467-490.

1982 THORNBROUGH, Emma Lou. "Booker T. Washington as Seen by His White Contemporaries." *J Neg Hist,* LIII (1968), 160-182.

1983 THORNBROUGH, Emma Lou. "The National Afro-American League, 1887-1908." *J S Hist,* XXVII (1961), 494-512.

1984 THORNBROUGH, Emma Lou. *The Negro in Indiana: A Study of a Minority.* Indianapolis, 1957.

1985 THORNBROUGH, Emma Lou. *A Short History of Indiana Negroes.* Indianapolis, 1963.

1986 THORNBROUGH, Emma Lou, ed. *Booker T. Washington.* Englewood Cliffs, N.J., 1969.†

1987 TINDALL, George S. "The Campaign for the Disfranchisement of Negroes in South Carolina." *J S Hist*, XV (1949), 212-234.

1988 TINDALL, George S. "The Liberian Exodus of 1878." *S C Hist Mag*, LIII (1952), 133-145.

1989 TINDALL, George S. *South Carolina Negroes, 1877-1901.* Columbia, S.C., 1952.†

1990 TUTTLE, William M., Jr. "Labor Conflict and Racial Violence: The Black Worker in Chicago, 1894-1919." *Labor Hist*, X (1969), 408-432.

1991 UROFSKY, Melvin I. "Blanche K. Bruce, United States Senator, 1875-1881." *J Miss Hist*, XXIX (1967), 118-141.

1992 UYA, Okon Edet. *From Slavery to Public Service; Robert Smalls, 1839-1915.* New York, 1971.†

1993 WARREN, Robert Penn. *Segregation: The Inner Conflict in the South.* New York, 1956.†

1994 WASHINGTON, Booker T. *Up from Slavery: An Autobiography.* Garden City, N.Y., 1900.†

1995 WASHINGTON, E. Davidson, ed. *Selected Speeches of Booker T. Washington.* Garden City, N.Y., 1932.

1996 WHARTON, Vernon Lane. *The Negro in Mississippi, 1865-1890.* Chapel Hill, 1947.†

1997 WILHOIT, Francis M. "An Interpretation of Populism's Impact on the Georgia Negro." See 706.

1998 WILLIAMS, Frank B., Jr. "The Poll Tax as a Suffrage Requirement in the South, 1870-1901." *J S Hist*, XVIII (1952), 469-496.

1999 WILLIAMSON, Joel. *After Slavery: The Negro in South Carolina during Reconstruction.* Chapel Hill, 1965.†

2000 WOODWARD, C. Vann. *Origins of the New South.* See 710.†

2001 WOODWARD, C. Vann. *The Strange Career of Jim Crow.* 2d ed. New York, 1966.†

2002 WOODWARD, C. Vann. "Tom Watson and the Negro." See 712.

2003 WYNES, Charles E. *Race Relations in Virginia, 1870-1902.* Charlottesville, Va., 1971.

7. Women

2004 ABBOTT, Edith. *Women in Industry. A Study in American Economic History.* New York, 1910.

2005 ADDAMS, Jane. *My Friend Julia Lathrop.* New York, 1935.

2006 ADDAMS, Jane. *Twenty Years at Hull-House.* See 1475.†

2007 BAYLES, G. J. *Women and the Law.* New York, 1901.

2008 BLACKWELL, A. S. *Lucy Stone, Pioneer of Woman's Rights.* Boston, 1930.

2009 BLACKWELL, Elizabeth. *Pioneer Work in Opening the Medical Profession to Women.* London and New York, 1895.

2010 BRACKETT, A. C. *Woman and Higher Education.* New York, 1893.

2011 BRUCE, H. A. *Woman in the Making of America.* Boston, 1928.

2012 CAMPBELL, H. S. *Women Wage-Earners.* Boston, 1893.

2013 CATT, C. C., and N. R. SHULER. *Woman Suffrage and Politics.* New York, 1923.†

2014 DORR, R. C. *Susan B. Anthony.* New York, 1928.

2015 DUFFUS, R. L. *Lillian Wald, Neighbor and Crusader.* New York, 1938.

2016 EARHART, Mary. *Frances Willard.* Chicago, 1944.

2017 FARRELL, John C. *Beloved Lady: A History of Jane Addams' Ideas on Reform and Peace.* Baltimore, 1967.

2018 FAWCETT, Millicent G. *Women's Suffrage.* London, 1912.

2019 FLEXNER, Eleanor. *Century of Struggle: The Women's Rights Movement in the United States.* Cambridge, Mass., 1959.†

2020 FOWLER, William W. *Women on the American Frontier.* Hartford, Conn., 1878

2021 GILMAN, Charlotte Perkins. *Women and Economics.* Boston, 1898.†

2022 GOLDMARK, Josephine. *Impatient Crusader; Florence Kelley's Life Story.* Urbana, Ill., 1953.

2023 GOUGH, J. B. *Platform Echoes.* Hartford, Conn., 1885.

2024 GROVES, E. R. *American Woman.* New York, 1944.

2025 HARPER, I. H. *Life and Work of Susan B. Anthony.* 3 vols. Indianapolis, 1898-1908.

2026 HIGGINSON, T. W. *Common Sense about Women.* New York, 1881.

2027 KRADITOR, Aileen S. *The Ideas of the Woman Suffrage Movement, 1890-1920.* New York, 1965.

2028 LIVERMORE, M. A. *Story of My Life.* Hartford, Conn., 1897.

2029 LUTZ, Alma. *Created Equal* [Elizabeth Cady Stanton]. New York, 1940.

2030 O'NEILL, William L. *The Woman Movement: Feminism in the United States and England.* London, 1969.

2031 PALMER, G. H. *The Life of Alice Freeman Palmer.* Boston, 1908.

2032 PANKHURST, Emmeline. *My Own Story.* New York, 1914.

2033 PECK, M. G. *Carrie C. Catt.* New York, 1944.

2034 PICK, Mary G. *Carrie Chapman Catt: A Biography.* New York, 1944.

2035 RICHARDS, L. E., and M. H. ELLIOTT. *Julia Ward Howe.* 2 vols. Boston, 1916.

2036 RICHARDSON, Dorothy. *The Long Day: The True Story of a New York Working Girl as Told by Herself.* New York, 1905.

2037 SMUTS, Robert W. *Women and Work in America.* New York, 1959.

2038 STANTON, Elizabeth Cady. *Eighty Years and More (1815-1897).* New York, 1898.

2039 STANTON, Elizabeth Cady, Susan B. ANTHONY, Matilda J. GAGE, and Ida H. HARPER. *History of Woman Suffrage.* 12 vols. New York, 1881-1922.

2040 STRACHEY, R. C. *Frances Willard.* London, 1912.

2041 SWISSHELM, Jane Grey. *Half a Century.* Chicago, 1880.

2042 TAYLOR, A. Elizabeth. "The Woman Suffrage Movement in Mississippi, 1890-1920." *J Miss Hist*, XXX (1968), 1-34.

2043 WALD, Lillian D. *The House on Henry Street.* New York, 1915.†

2044 WILLARD, Frances E. *Glimpses of Fifty Years; the Autobiography of an American Woman.* 2 vols. Chicago, 1889.

2045 WILLARD, Frances E., and M. A. LIVERMORE, eds. *American Woman.* New York, 1897.

2046 *Women in Gainful Occupations, 1870-1920.* Census Monograph, IX. Washington, D.C., 1929.

XV. The New South

2047 ARMES, Ethel. *Story of Coal and Iron in Alabama.* Birmingham, Ala., 1910.

2048 BARROWS, Walter M. *The New South.* New York, 1884.

2049 BROOKS, Eugene C. *Story of Cotton and the Development of the Cotton States.* Chicago and New York, 1911.

2050 BRUCE, Philip Alexander. *The Rise of the New South.* Philadelphia, 1905.

2051 CASH, Wilbur J. *The Mind of the South.* New York, 1941.†

2052 CAUTHEN, Charles Edward, ed. *Family Letters of the Three Wade Hamptons, 1782-1901.* Columbia, S.C., 1953.

2053 CHANDLER, A. C., et al. "Economic History, 1865-1900." *The South in the Building of the Nation.* Richmond, Va., 1909.

2054 CLARK, Thomas D. "The Post-Civil War Economy in the South." *Am Jew Hist Q*, LV (1966), 424-433.

2055 CLARK, Thomas. D. *The Southern Country Editor.* Indianapolis, 1948.

2056 CLARK, Thomas D., ed. *Travels in the New South.* 2 vols. Norman, Okla., 1962.

2057 CLARK, Thomas D., and Albert D. KIRWAN. *The South since Appomattox.* New York, 1967.

2058 EMORY, Quinter. *Economic History of the South.* New York, 1934.

2059 EZELL, John S. *The South since 1865.* New York, 1963.

2060 FROST, William Goodell. "Our Contemporary Ancestors in Southern Mountains." *Atl Month,* LXXXIII (1899), 311-319.

2061 GASTON, Paul M. *The New South Creed, a Study in Southern Mythmaking.* New York, 1970.

2062 GRADY, Henry W. "Cotton and Its Kingdom." *Har Mag,* LXIII (1881), 719-734.

2063 HILLYARD, M. B. *New South: Its Resources and Attractions.* Baltimore, 1887.

2064 JOHNSTON, John Warfield. *Emancipation of Southern Whites and Its Effect upon Both Races.* Baltimore, 1887.

2065 KELLEY, W. D. *The Old South and the New.* New York, 1888.

2066 MC CLURE, Alexander K. *The South: Its Industrial, Financial, and Political Condition.* Philadelphia, 1886.

2067 MC PHERSON, James M. "Coercion or Conciliation? Abolitionists Debate President Hayes's Southern Policy." See 384.

2068 MIMS, Edwin D. *The Advancing South.* Garden City, N.Y., 1926.

2069 MITCHELL, Broadus. *The Rise of Cotton Mills in the South.* See 1254.

2070 MITCHELL, Broadus, and George S. MITCHELL. *The Industrial Revolution in the South.* Baltimore, 1931.

2071 NIXON, Raymond B. *Henry B. Grady, Spokesman of the New South.* New York, 1943.

2072 SELLERS, Charles G., ed. *The Southerner as American.* Chapel Hill, 1960.†

2073 SIMKINS, Francis B. *A History of the South.* 3d ed. New York, 1963.

2074 SIMKINS, Francis B. *Pitchfork Ben Tillman, South Carolinian.* See 206.†

2075 STILES, C. W. *Report upon Prevalence and Geographic Distribution of Hookworm Disease in the United States.* Washington, D.C., 1903.

2076 THOMPSON, Holland. *From the Cotton Field to the Cotton Mill.* New York, 1906.

2077 THOMPSON, Holland. *The New South: A Chronicle of Social and Industrial Revolution.* New Haven, 1919.

2078 VANDIVER, Frank E., ed. *The Idea of the South.* Chicago, 1964.

2079 WARREN, Robert Penn. *The Legacy of the Civil War.* New York, 1961.†

2080 WOODWARD, C. Vann. *The Burden of Southern History.* Baton Rouge, 1960.†

2081 WOODWARD, C. Vann. *Origins of the New South.* See 710.†

2082 WOODWARD, C. Vann. *Reunion and Reaction: The Compromise of 1877 and the End of Reconstruction.* See 440.†

2083 WOODWARD, C. Vann. *Tom Watson: Agrarian Rebel.* See 228.†

XVI. The Last West

1. General

2084 ALBRIGHT, Robert Erwin. "Western Statehood Movement." *Pac Hist Rev*, III (1934), 296-306.

2085 ANDERSON, Nels. *Desert Saints*. Chicago, 1942.†

2086 ARRINGTON, Leonard J. *Great Basin Kingdom; an Economic History of the Latter Day Saints*. Cambridge, Mass., 1958.†

2087 ATHEARN, Robert G. "A Brahmin in Buffaloland." *W Hist Q*, I (1970), 21-34.　·

2088 BAILY, M. L. T. "Prairie Homesteading." *Palimpsest*, XXIII (1942), 229-238.

2089 BARNARD, Evan G. *Rider of Cherokee Strip*. Boston, 1936.

2090 BILLINGTON, Ray Allen. *America's Frontier Heritage*. New York, 1966.†

2091 BILLINGTON, Ray Allen. "The Frontier and I." *W Hist Q*, I (1970), 5-20.

2092 BILLINGTON, Ray Allen. *Westward Expansion*. 3d ed. New York, 1967.†

2093 BLAKE, Charles T. "Working for Wells Fargo, 1860-1863." *Calif Hist Soc Q*, XVI (1937), 30, 172-181.

2094 BOGUE, Allan G., Thomas D. PHILLIPS, and James E. WRIGHT, eds., *The West of the American People*. Itasca, Ill., 1970.†

2095 BOWMAN, Isaiah. *The Pioneer Fringe*. New York, 1931.

2096 BRANCH, Edward Douglas. *Westward*. New York and London, 1950.

2097 BRANDT, R. O. "Prairie Pioneering." *Nor Am Stud Rec*, VII (1933), 1-46.

2098 BRIGGS, Harold E. "Early Freight and Stage Lines in Dakota." *N D Hist Q*, III (1928-1929), 229—261.

2099 BRIGGS, Harold E. *Frontier of the Northwest: A History of the Upper Missouri Valley*. New York, 1940.

2100 BROCKETT, Linus Pierpont. *Our Western Empire*. Philadelphia, 1881.

2101 BROWN, Elmer E. "No Man's Land." *Chron Okla*, IV (1926), 89-99.

2102 BURLINGAME, Merrill Gildea. *Montana Frontier*. Helena, Mont., 1942.

2103 CAUGHEY, John Walton. *History of the Pacific Coast*. New York, 1938.

2104 CHAPMAN, Arthur. *Pony Express*. New York, 1932.

2105 CLARK, Thomas. *Frontier America: The Story of the Westward Movement*. New York, 1969.

2106 DARRAH, William C. *Powell of the Colorado*. Princeton, 1951.

2107 DICK, Everett. *The Law of the Land: A Social History of the Public Lands from the Articles of Confederation to the New Deal.* Lincoln, Neb., 1970.

2108 DICK, Everett. *The Sod-House Frontier.* See 1625.

2109 DICK, Everett. "Water, a Frontier Problem." *Neb Hist,* XLIX (1968), 215-245.

2110 DIMSDALE, Thomas Josiah. *Vigilantes of Montana, or Popular Justice in the Rocky Mountains.* 2d ed. Virginia City, Mont., 1882.

2111 DODGE, R. I. *Plains of Great West, and Their Inhabitants.* New York, 1877.

2112 DUNHAM, Harold H. "Crucial Years of General Land Office." *Ag Hist,* XI (1937), 117-141.

2113 DUNIWAY, Abigail Scott. *From the West to the West.* Chicago, 1905.

2114 FITE, Gilbert C. "History and Historians of the Great Plains." *N D Q,* XXXIV (1966), 89-95.

2115 FORMAN, Grant. *A History of Oklahoma.* Norman, Okla., 1942.

2116 FRY, F. *Fry's Traveler's Guide, and Descriptive Journal of the Great Northwestern Territories of the United States of America.* Cincinnati, 1865.

2117 GANOE, John T. "Beginnings of Irrigation." *Miss Val Hist Rev,* XXV (1938), 59-78.

2118 GARDNER, Hamilton. "Communism among Mormons." *Q J Econ,* XXXVII (1922), 134-174.

2119 GARDNER, Hamilton. "Cooperation among Mormons." *Q J Econ,* XXXI (1917), 261-499.

2120 GATES, Paul W. "The Homestead Act in an Incongruous Land System." *Am Hist Rev,* XLI (1936), 652-681.

2121 GILBERT, Frank T. *Resources, Business, and Business Men of Montana.* Walla Walla, Wash., 1888.

2122 GITTINGER, Roy. *The Formation of the State of Oklahoma.* Berkeley, 1917.

2123 GOULDER, William Armistead. *Reminiscences.* Boise, Idaho, 1909.

2124 HAFEN, LeRoy R., ed. *Pike's Peak Guide Books of 1859.* Glendale, Calif., 1941.

2125 HAGEDORN, Hermann. *Roosevelt in the Bad Lands.* Boston and New York, 1921.

2126 HALL, Edward Hepple. *Great West.* New York, 1864.

2127 HARLOW, Alvin F. *Old Waybills.* New York, 1934.

2128 HAYTER, E. W. "Barbed Wire Fencing." *Ag Hist,* XIII (1939), 189-207.

2129 HEBARD, Grace Raymond, and E. A. BRININSTOOL. *Bozeman Trail.* Cleveland, 1922.

2130 HIBBARD, Benjamin H. *A History of the Public Land Policies.* 2d ed. Madison, 1965.†

2131 HICKS, John D. *The Constitutions of the Northwest States.* Lincoln, Neb., 1923.

2132 HICKS, John D. "The Development of Civilization in the Middle West, 1860-1900." *Sources of Culture in the Middle West: Backgrounds versus Frontiers.* Ed. Dixon Ryan Fox. New York, 1934.

2133 HINTON, Richard I. *Handbook to Arizona.* San Francisco, 1878.

2134 HIRSHON, Stanley P. *The Lion of the Lord: A Biography of Brigham Young.* New York, 1959.

2135 HOUGH, Emerson. *The Passing of the Frontier, Chronicle of the Old West.* New Haven, 1921.

2136 HUMPHREY, Seth K. "Rushing the Cherokee Strip." *Atl Month,* CXLVII (1931), 566-577.

2137 HUNGERFORD, Edward. *Wells Fargo, Advancing the American Frontier.* New York, 1949.

2138 IDE, L. A. "In a Prairie Schooner." *Wash Hist Q,* XVIII (1927), 122-131, 191-198, 277-288.

2139 JONES, William Albert. *Report upon Reconnaissance of Northwestern Wyoming.* Washington, D.C., 1875.

2140 JORDAN, D. S. "California and the Californians." *Atl Month,* LXXXII (1898), 793-801.

2141 KING, Clarence. *Mountaineering in Sierra Nevada.* Boston, 1872.

2142 KINNEY, Jay P. *The Development of Forest Law in America.* New York, 1917.

2143 LAMPHERE, George N. "History of Wheat Raising in the Red River Valley." *Coll Minneapolis His Soc* (1900), Part I, 1-33.

2144 LANGFORD, Nathaniel Pitt. *Vigilante Days and Ways.* Chicago, 1912.

2145 LARSON, Gustive O. "The Story of the Perpetual Emigration Fund." *Miss Val Hist Rev,* XVIII (1931), 184-194.

2146 MC CALLUM, Henry D., and Frances T. MC CALLUM. *The Wire that Fenced the West.* Norman, Okla., 1965.

2147 MC CLURE, Alexander K. *Three Thousand Miles through Rocky Mountains.* Philadelphia, 1869.

2148 MC DERMOTT, John F., ed. *Travelers on the Western Frontier.* Urbana, Ill., 1970.

2149 MAGUIRE, Henry N. *New Map and Guide to Dakota and Black Hills.* Chicago, 1877.

2150 MAGUIRE, Henry N., and H. HORR. *Historical Sketch and Essay on Resources of Montana.* Helena, Mont., 1868.

2151 MAJORS, Alexander. *Seventy Years on the Frontier.* New ed. Columbus, Ohio, 1950.

2152 MALIN, James C. *The Grasslands of North America.* Lawrence, Kan., 1947.

2153 MASLIN, E. W., ed. *Resources of California.* Sacramento, 1893.

2154 MATHEWS, Mary M. *Ten Years in Nevada.* Buffalo, N.Y., 1880.

2155 MEINIG, D. W. *The Great Columbia Plain: A Historical Geography, 1805-1910.* Seattle, 1968.

2156 MILAN, Joe B. "Opening of Cherokee Outlet." *Chron Okla,* IX (1931), 268-286, 454-475.

2157 MILLER, William H. *The History of Kansas City.* Kansas City, Mo., 1881.

2158 MOFFITT, James W. "Diary of an Eighty-Niner." *Chron Okla,* XV (1937), 66-69.

2159 MORRIS, Ralph C. "The Notion of a Great American Desert East of the Rockies." *Miss Val Hist Rev,* XIII (1926), 190-200.

2160 MULLAN, John. *Miners' and Travelers' Guide to Oregon, Washington, Idaho, Montana, Wyoming and Colorado.* New York, 1865.

2161 NEWELL, Frederick H. *Report on Agriculture by Irrigation.* Washington, D.C., 1894.

2162 ONDERDONK, James Laurence. *Idaho.* San Francisco, 1885.

2163 ORPEN, E. R. *Old Emigrant Days in Kansas.* New York, 1928.

2164 PAUL, Rodman W. "The Mormons as a Theme in Western Historical Writing." *J Am Hist,* LIV (1967), 511-523.

2165 PAXSON, Frederic L. "Admission of Omnibus States." *Wis Hist Soc Proc* (1911), 77-96.

2166 PAXSON, Frederic L. *Last American Frontier.* New York, 1910.

2167 PERRY, Dan W. "Colonel Crocker and the Boomer Movement." *Chron Okla,* XIII (1935), 273-296.

2168 PERRY, Dan W. "First Two Years." *Chron Okla,* VII (1929), 278-322, 419-457.

2169 POMEROY, Earl S. *In Search of the Golden West: The Tourists in Western America.* New York, 1957.

2170 POMEROY, Earl S. *The Pacific Slope: A History of California, Oregon, Washington, Idaho, Utah, and Nevada.* New York, 1965.

2171 POMEROY, Earl S. *The Territories and the United States, 1861-1890.* Philadelphia, 1947.†

2172 PORTER, R. P. *The West: From the Census of 1880.* Chicago, 1882.

2173 POWELL, John Wesley. "Institutions for Arid Lands." *Cent Mag,* XL (1890), 111-116.

2174 POWELL, John Wesley. *Report on Lands of Arid Region.* Washington, D.C., 1879.

2175 QUIETT, Glenn Chesney. *They Built the West.* New York, 1934.

2176 RAE, William Fraser. *Westward by Rail.* London, 1871.

2177 RALPH, Julian. *Our Great West.* New York, 1893.

2178 REMINGTON, Frederic. *Pony Tracks*. New York, 1895.

2179 RICHARDSON, Albert Deane. *Our New States and Territories*. New York, 1866.

2180 RICHARDSON, Rupert Norval, and Carl Coke RISTER. *Greater Southwest*. Glendale, Calif., 1934.

2181 RISTER, Carl Coke. *Land Hunger: David L. Payne and the Oklahoma Boomers*. Norman, Okla., 1942.

2182 RISTER, Carl Coke. *Southern Plainsmen*. Norman, Okla., 1938.

2183 ROBBINS, Roy M. *Our Landed Heritage: The Public Domain, 1776-1936*. Princeton, 1942.

2184 ROBBINS, Roy M. "The Public Domain in an Era of Exploitation, 1862-1901." *Ag Hist*, XIII (1939), 97-118.

2185 ROBINSON, Edward Van Dyke. *Early Economic Conditions and Agriculture in Minnesota*. Minneapolis, 1915.

2186 ROOT, Frank A., and W. B. CONNELLEY. *Overland Stage to California*. Topeka, Kan., 1901.

2187 ROSS, N. W. *Westward the Women*. New York, 1945.

2188 ROWBOTHAM, Francis J. *Trip to Prairie-Land*. London, 1885.

2189 RUEDE, Howard. *Sod-House Days*. New York, 1937.

2190 RUMFIELD, Hiram S. "Letters of Overland Mail Agent in Utah." *Proc Am Ant Soc*, XXXVIII (1928), pt. 2, 227-302.

2191 SHANNON, Fred A. *The Farmers' Last Frontier: Agriculture, 1860-1897*. See 658.†

2192 SHARP, Paul F. *Whoop-Up County: The Canadian-American West, 1865-1885*. Minneapolis, 1955.

2193 SHATRAW, Milton. *Thrashin' Time, Memories of a Montana Boyhood*. Palo Alto, Calif., 1968.

2194 SMITH, Emily B. "The Status of Provisional Governments in Oklahoma." *S W Soc Sci Q*, XIII (1933), 353-367.

2195 SMITH, Henry Nash. *Virgin Land: The American West as Symbol and Myth*. Cambridge, Mass., 1950.†

2196 SPRING, Agnes Wright. *Colorado Charley, Wild Bill's Pard*. Boulder, Colo., 1968.

2197 STECKMESSER, Kent. *The Western Hero in History and Legend*. Norman, Okla., 1965.

2198 STEGNER, Wallace. *Beyond the Hundredth Meridian: John Wesley Powell and the Second Opening of the West*. Boston, 1954.†

2199 STRAHORN, Carrie Adellgreen. *Fifteen Thousand Miles by Stage*. New York, 1911.

2200 STRAHORN, Robert Edmund. *Handbook of Wyoming and Guide to the Black Hills and Big Horn Regions, for Citizen, Emigrant, and Tourist*. Chicago, 1877.

2201 STRAHORN, Robert Edmund. *Resources and Attractions of Idaho Territory.* Boise City, Idaho, 1881.

2202 TAFT, Robert. *Artists and Illustrators of the Old West, 1850-1900.* New York, 1969.

2203 THAYER, William M. *Marvels of the New West.* Norwich, Conn., 1887.

2204 THOMAS, George. *Development of Institutions under Irrigation.* New York, 1920.

2205 THOMPSON, C. W. "Movement of Wheat Growing." *Q J Econ,* XVIII (1904), 570-584.

2206 TILDEN, Freeman. *Following the Frontier with F. Jay Haynes: Pioneer Photographer of the Old West.* New York, 1964.

2207 TOWNE, Charles W., and Edward N. WENTWORTH. *Shepherd's Empire.* Norman, Okla., 1945.

2208 TWAIN, Mark. *Roughing It.* (Various eds.)†

2209 ULPH, Owen. "The Legacy of the American Wild West in Medieval Scholarship." *Am West,* III (1966), 50-52, 88-91.

2210 Union Pacific Railroad. *Wealth and Resources of Oregon and Washington, the Pacific Northwest.* Portland, Ore., 1889.

2211 VICTOR, Frances F. *Atlantis Arisen.* Philadelphia, 1891.

2212 WARREN, Sidney. *Farthest Frontier: The Pacific Northwest.* New York, 1949.

2213 WEBB, Walter Prescott. *The Great Plains.* Boston, 1931.

2214 WHITE, Lynn, Jr. "The Legacy of the Middle Ages in the American Wild West." *Am West,* III (1966), 73-79, 95.

2215 WICKES, Hamilton S. "Opening of Oklahoma." *Chron Okla,* IV (1926), 129-142.

2216 WILKINS, Thurman. *Clarence King, a Biography.* New York, 1958.

2217 WILTSEE, Ernest A. *Pioneer Miner and the Pack Mule Express.* San Francisco, 1931.

2218 WINTHER, Oscar O. "English Migration to the American West, 1865-1900." *Hunt Lib Q,* XXVII (1964), 159-173.

2219 WINTHER, Oscar O. *The Great Northwest.* New York, 1950.

2220 WINTHER, Oscar. *Via Western Express and Stagecoach.* Stanford, 1945.†

2221 WOOD, Stanley. *Over the Range to the Golden Gate.* Chicago, 1889.

2222 WRIGHT, Robert M. *Dodge City.* Wichita, Kan., 1913.

2223 WYMAN, Walter D. "Western Folklore and History." *Am West,* I (1964), 45-51.

2224 WYMAN, Walter D., and Clifton B. KROEBER, eds. *The Frontier in Perspective.* Madison, 1957.†

2225 YOUNG, Francis C. *Across the Plains in '65.* Denver, 1905.

2. Natural Resources

2226 CAMERON, Julius B. *The Development of Governmental Forest Control.* Baltimore, 1928.

2227 CATHER, Willa. *My Antonia.* Boston and New York, 1918.†

2228 CATHER, Willa. *O Pioneers!* Boston and New York, 1913.†

2229 CHANCE, Henry M. "Report on the Mining Methods and Appliances Used in the Anthracite Coal Fields." *Second Geological Survey of Pennsylvania: 1883.* Harrisburg, Pa., 1883.

2230 DICK, Everett. *The Sod-House Frontier, 1854-1890.* See 1625.

2231 DONALDSON, Thomas C. *The Public Domain. Its History with Statistics.* Washington, D.C., 1881.

2232 DUNHAM, Harold H. *Government Handout: A Study in the Administration of the Public Lands.* New York, 1941.

2233 EAVENSON, Howard N. *The First Century and a Quarter of the American Coal Industry.* Baltimore, 1942.

2234 FRIES, Robert F. *Empire in Pine: The Story of Lumbering in Wisconsin, 1830-1900.* Madison, 1951.

2235 GANOE, J. T. "Desert Land Act in Operation." *Ag Hist,* XI (1937), 142-157.

2236 GANOE, J. T. "The Origin of a National Reclamation Policy." *Miss Val Hist Rev,* XVIII (1931), 34-52.

2237 GATES, Paul W. *The Wisconsin Pine Lands of Cornell University: A Study in Land Policy and Absentee Ownership.* Ithaca, N.Y., 1943.

2238 HATCHER, Harlan. *The Great Lakes.* New York, 1944.

2239 HATCHER, Harlan. *Lake Erie.* Indianapolis, 1945.

2240 HESS, R. H. "Beginnings of Irrigation." *J Pol Econ,* XX (1912), 807-833.

2241 ISE, John. *The United States Forest Policy.* New Haven, 1920.

2242 ISE, John. *The United States Oil Policy.* New Haven, 1926.

2243 LAMAR, Howard Roberts. *Dakota Territory, 1861-1889: A Study of Frontier Politics.* See 841.†

2244 LARSON, Agnes M. *History of the White Pine Industry in Minnesota.* Minneapolis, 1949.

2245 MUSSEY, Henry R. *Combination in the Mining Industry. A Study of Concentration in Lake Superior Iron Ore Production.* New York, 1905.

2246 PARKER, Edward W. "Coal-Cutting Machinery." *Tran Am Inst Min Engr,* XXIX (1899), 405-459.

2247 PARSONS, Arthur B., ed. *Seventy-five Years of Progress in the Mining Industry.* New York, 1947.

2248 PINCHOT, Gifford. *Breaking New Ground.* New York, 1947.

2249 RANEY, W. F. "Timber Culture Acts." *Proc Miss Val Hist Assoc,* X (1921), 219-229.

2250 RECTOR, William G. *Log Transportation in the Lake States Lumber Industry, 1840-1918.* Glendale, Calif., 1953.

2251 RODGERS, Andrew D., III. *Bernhard Eduard Fernow: A Story of North American Forestry.* Princeton, 1951.

2252 ROLVAAG, Ole. *Giants in the Earth.* New York and London, 1929.†

2253 SAKOLSKI, Aaron Morton. *The Great American Land Bubble.* New York and London, 1932.

2254 SANDOZ, Mari. *Old Jules.* Boston, 1935.†

2255 SCHENK, Carl A. *The Biltmore Story: Recollections of the Beginning of Forestry in the United States.* St. Paul, 1955.

2256 STEPHENSON, Isaac. *Recollections of a Long Life: 1829-1915.* Chicago, 1915.

2257 WIRTH, Fremont P. *The Discovery and Exploitation of the Minnesota Iron Lands.* Cedar Rapids, Iowa, 1937.

3. Cattle Kingdom

2258 ADAMS, Andy. *Log of a Cowboy; A Narrative of the Old Trail Days.* New York and Boston, 1903.†

2259 ALDRIDGE, Reginald. *Life on a Ranch; Ranch Notes in Kansas, Colorado, the Indian Territory, and Northern Texas.* New York, 1884.

2260 ATHERTON, Lewis. *The Cattle Kings.* Bloomington, 1961.

2261 BAUMANN, John. "On a Western Ranch." *Fortnightly Rev,* XLVII, Old Ser. (1887), 516-533.

2262 BENTLEY, Henry L. "Cattle Ranges of Southwest." *Farmer's Bull Dept Ag,* No. 72 (1898), 1-31.

2263 BRANCH, Edward Douglas. *The Cowboy and His Interpreters.* New York, 1926.

2264 BRIGGS, Harold. "The Development and Decline of Open Range Ranching in the Northwest." *Miss Val Hist Rev,* XX (1934), 521-536.

2265 BRISBIN, James Sanks. *Beef Bonanza.* Norman, Okla., 1959.

2266 BRONSON, Edgar Beecher. *Reminiscences of a Ranchman.* New York, 1908.†

2267 BURLINGAME, Merrill G. *The Montana Frontier.* Helena, Mont., 1942.

2268 CARMAN, Ezra, et al. *Special Report of the History and Present Condition of the Sheep Industry of the United States.* Washington, D.C., 1892.

2269 CAULEY, Troy Jesse. "Early Business Methods in Texas Cattle Industry." *J Econ Bus Hist,* IV (1932), 461-486.

2270 CAWELTI, John G. "Cowboys, Indians, Outlaws." *Am West,* I (1964), 29-35, 77-78.

2271 CLAY, John. *My Life on the Range.* Chicago, 1924.

2272 DALE, Edward Everett. *Cow Country.* Norman, Okla., 1942.

2273 DALE, Edward Everett. "The Ranchman's Last Frontier." *Miss Val Hist Rev*, X (1923), 34-46.

2274 DALE, Edward Everett. *The Range Cattle Industry.* Norman, Okla., 1930.

2275 DICK, Everett. "The Long Drive." *Coll Kan State Hist Soc*, XVII (1926), 27-97.

2276 DOBIE, James Frank. *Longhorns.* Boston, 1941.†

2277 DURHAM, Philip, and Everett L. JONES. *The Negro Cowboy.* See 1905.

2278 FLETCHER, R. S. "End of the Open Range in Eastern Montana." *Miss Val Hist Rev*, XIV (1929), 188-211.

2279 FRANTZ, Joe Bertram, and Julian Ernest CHOATE. *The American Cowboy: The Myth and the Reality.* Norman, Okla., 1955.

2280 FRANTZ, Joe B. "Hoof and Horn on the Chisholm Trail." *Am West*, IV (1967), 15-20, 70-71.

2281 FRENCH, William. *Some Recollections of a Western Ranchman; New Mexico, 1883-1899.* New York, 1928.

2282 GARD, Wayne. *The Chisholm Trail.* Norman, Okla., 1954.

2283 GARD, Wayne. *Frontier Justice.* Norman, Okla., 1949.

2284 GRESSLEY, Gene M. *Bankers and Cattlemen.* New York, 1966.†

2285 GRINNELL, Joseph B. "Cattle Interests West of the Mississippi," *Rep Bur Animal Indus*, I (1884), 233-244.

2286 HASKETT, Bert. "Early History of the Cattle Industry in Arizona." *Ariz Hist Rev*, VI (1935), 3-42.

2287 HENDERSON, James C. "Reminiscences of a Range Rider." *Chron Okla*, III (1925), 253-288.

2288 HOLDEN, William Curry. *Alkali Trails; or, Social and Economic Movements of the Texas Frontier, 1846-1900.* Dallas, 1930.

2289 HOUGH, Emerson. *The Story of the Cowboy.* New York, 1897.

2290 HUNTER, John Marvin, ed. *The Trail Drivers of Texas.* San Antonio, 1925.

2291 JAQUES, Mary J. *Texas Ranch Life.* London, 1894.

2292 KENNEDY, Michael S., ed. *Cowboys and Cattlemen: A Roundup from Montana, the Magazine of Western History.* New York, 1964.

2293 LINDSAY, Charles. *The Big Horn Basin.* Lincoln, Neb., 1932.

2294 LOVE, Clara M. "Cattle Industry in the Southwest." *S W Hist Q*, XIX (1916), 370-399.

2295 MC COY, Joseph G. *The Cattle Trade of the West and Southwest.* Ann Arbor, 1874.

2296 MORRISEY, Richard J. "The Early Range Cattle Industry in Arizona." *Ag Hist*, XXIV (1950), 151-156.

2297 OLIPHANT, James O. "History of Livestock Industry in the Pacific Northwest." *Ore Hist Q,* XLIX (1948), 3-29.

2298 OLIPHANT, James O. *On the Cattle Ranges of the Oregon Country.* Seattle, 1968.

2299 OSGOOD, Ernest Staples. *The Day of the Cattleman.* Minneapolis, 1929.†

2300 PEAKE, Ora Brooks. *The Colorado Range Industry.* Glendale, Calif., 1937.

2301 PELZER, Louis. "A Cattleman's Commonwealth on the Western Range." *Miss Val Hist Rev,* XIII (1926), 30-49.

2302 PELZER, Louis. *The Cattleman's Frontier.* Glendale, Calif., 1936.

2303 PHILLIPS, Rufus. "Early Cowboy Life in the Arkansas Valley." *Colo Mag,* VII (1930), 165-179.

2304 POWELL, Fred W. *Bureau of Animal Industry, Its History, Activities and Organization.* Baltimore, 1927.

2305 RIDINGS, Sam P. *Chisholm Trail.* Guthrie, Okla., 1936.

2306 ROLLINS, Philip Ashton. *The Cowboy, His Characteristics, His Equipment, and His Part in the Development of the West.* New York, 1936.

2307 ROOSEVELT, Theodore. *Ranch Life and the Hunting Trail.* Ann Arbor, 1888.

2308 SHEPHERD, William. *Prairie Experiences in Handling Cattle and Sheep.* London, 1884.

2309 STREETER, Floyd Benjamin. *Prairie Trails and Cow Towns: The Opening of the Old West.* New York, 1963.

2310 TANBERG, Frank. "Cowboy Life on the Open Range of Northeastern Colorado." *Colo Mag,* XII (1935), 23-28.

2311 TAYLOR, H. M. "Condition of the Cattle-Range Industry." *Rep Bur Animal Indus* (1886), 105-124.

2312 TAYLOR, H. M. "Importance of the Range Industry." *Rep Bur Animal Indus* (1885), 293-325.

2313 TAYLOR, Thomas U. *The Chisholm Trail and Other Routes.* San Antonio, 1936.

2314 TAYLOR, Thomas U. *Jesse Chisholm.* Bandera, Tex., 1939.

2315 VON RICHTHOFEN, Walter. *Cattle Raising on the Plains of North America.* Norman, Okla., 1964.

2316 WELLMAN, Paul I. *The Trampling Herd.* New York, 1939.

2317 WENTWORTH, Edward N. *America's Sheep Trails.* Ames, Iowa, 1948.

2318 WILKESON, Frank. "Cattle Raising on the Plains." *Har Mag,* LXXII (1886), 788-795.

4. Mining

2319 ANDERSON, Alexander Dwight. *The Silver Country; or, The Great Southwest.* New York, 1877.

2320 ATHEARN, Lewis. "The Mining Promoter in the Trans-Mississippi West." *W Hist Q*, I (1970), 35-50.

2321 BRIGGS, Harold E. "The Black Hills Gold Rush." *N D Hist Q*, V (1931), 71-99.

2322 CHAPMAN, Arthur. *The Pony Express*. New York, 1932.

2323 COON, S. J. "The Influence of the Gold Camps and the Development of Western Montana." *J Pol Econ*, XXXVIII (1930), 580-599.

2324 FREDERICK, James Vincent. *Ben Holladay, the Stagecoach King.* Glendale, Calif., 1940.

2325 GREEVER, William S. *The Bonanza West: The Story of the Western Mining Rushes, 1848-1900.* Norman, Okla., 1963.

2326 HAFEN, LeRoy R. *The Overland Mail, 1849-1869*. Cleveland, 1926.

2327 HAFEN, LeRoy R., ed. *Colorado Gold Rush*. Glendale, Calif., 1941.

2328 HAFEN, LeRoy R., ed. *Overland Routes to Gold Fields, 1859*. Glendale, Calif., 1942.

2329 HILL, Jim Dan. "The Early Mining Camp in American Life." *Pac Hist Rev*, I (1932), 295-311.

2330 INGHAM, George T. *Digging Gold among the Rockies*. Philadelphia, 1880.

2331 JACKSON, W. Turentine. *Treasure Hill: Portrait of a Silver Mining Camp*. Tucson, 1963.

2332 LAMBIE, Joseph T. *From Mine to Market: The History of Coal Transportation on the Norfolk and Western Railway*. New York, 1954.

2333 LARSEN, Arthur T. "Black Hills Gold Rush." *N D Hist Q*, VI (1932), 302-318.

2334 LEWIS, Oscar. *Silver Kings: The Lives and Times of MacKay, Fair, Flood, and O'Brien, Lords of the Nevada Comstock Lode*. New York, 1947.

2335 LORD, Eliot. *Comstock Mining and Mines*. Berkeley, 1959. [Reprint of 1883 ed.]

2336 LYMAN, George Dunlop. *Ralston's Ring: California Plunders the Comstock Lode*. New York, 1937.

2337 LYMAN, George Dunlop. *The Saga of the Comstock Lode*. New York, 1934.

2338 MEAD, Edward Sherwood. *Story of Gold*. New York, 1915.

2339 MUSSEY, Henry Raymond. *Combination in the Mining Industry*. New York, 1905.

2340 PAUL, Rodman W. *California Gold: The Beginning of Mining in the Far West*. Cambridge, Mass., 1947.†

2341 PAUL, Rodman W. "Mining Frontiers as a Measure of Western Historical Writings." *Pac Hist Rev*, XXXIII (1964), 25-34.

2342 PAUL, Rodman W. *Mining Frontiers of the Far West, 1848-1880*. New York, 1963.†

2343 QUIETT, Glenn C. *Pay Dirt, a Panorama of American Gold Rushes.* New York, 1936.

2344 RICKARD, Thomas A. *A History of American Mining.* New York, 1932.

2345 RICKARD, Thomas A. *Man and Metals.* 2 vols. New York, 1932.

2346 SHINN, Charles Howard. *Mining Camps: A Study in American Frontier Government.* New York, 1885.

2347 SHINN, Charles Howard. *The Story of the Mine.* New York, 1896.

2348 SMITH, Duane A. *Rocky Mountain Mining Camps: The Urban Frontier.* See 1574.

2349 SMITH, Grant Horace. *The History of Comstock Lode, 1850-1920.* Reno, Nev., 1943.

2350 SPENCE, Clark C. *British Investments and the American Mining Frontier, 1860-1901.* Ithaca, N.Y., 1958.

2351 SPENCE, Clark C. *Mining Engineers and the American West: The Lace Boot Brigade (1849-1933).* New Haven, 1970.

2352 STOKES, George, and H. R. DRIGGS. *Deadwood Gold.* Chicago, 1926.

2353 STOLL, William T., and H. W. WHICKER. *Silver Strike.* Boston, 1932.

2354 TREXLER, Harrison Anthony. *Flour and Wheat in Montana Gold Camps.* Missoula, Mont., 1918.

2355 TRIMBLE, William J. *The Mining Advance into the Inland Empire.* Madison, 1914.

2356 TRIMBLE, William J. "A Reconsideration of Gold Discoveries in the Northwest." *Miss Val Hist Rev,* V (1918), 70-77.

2357 TWAIN, Mark. *Roughing It.* See 2208.†

2358 WALDORF, John Taylor. *A Kid on the Comstock.* Palo Alto, Calif., 1970.

2359 WILLISON, George F. *Here They Dug Gold.* New York, 1931.

2360 WILSON, Neill Compton. *Silver Stampede.* New York, 1937.

2361 WOLLE, Muriel Sibell. *Montana Pay Dirt: A Guide to the Mining Camps of the Treasure State.* Denver, 1963.

2362 WRIGHT, William. *The Big Bonanza.* New York, 1947.

2363 YOUNG, Lewis Emmanuel. *Mine Taxation in United States.* Urbana, Ill., 1917.

5. Indians

2364 ANDRIST, Ralph K. *The Long Death; The Last Days of the Plains Indians.* New York, 1964.†

2365 ARNOLD, Royal Ross. *Indian Wars of Idaho.* Caldwell, Idaho, 1932.

2366 ATHEARN, Robert G. *William Tecumseh Sherman and the Settlement of the West.* Norman, Okla., 1956.

2367 BARNES, Will C. "The Apaches' Last Stand in Arizona." *Ariz Hist Rev*, III (1930-1931), 36-59.

2368 BIRGE, Julius Charles. *The Awakening of the Desert*. Boston, 1912.

2369 BOURKE, John Gregory. *On the Border with Crook*. New York, 1891.

2370 BRANCH, Edward Douglas. *The Hunting of the Buffalo*. New York, 1929.

2371 BRIMLOW, George Francis. *The Bannock Indian War of 1878*. Caldwell, Idaho, 1938.

2372 BRININSTOOL, Earl Alonzo, et al. "Chief Crazy Horse: His Career and Death." *Neb Hist Mag*, XII (1929), 4-77.

2373 BROWN, Dee Alexander. *The Galvanized Yankees*. Urbana, Ill., 1963.

2374 BROWNE, John Ross. *Adventures in the Apache Country*. New York, 1869.

2375 BURLINGAME, Merrill G. "The Buffalo in Trade and Commerce." *N D Hist Q*, III (1929), 262-291.

2376 CAMPBELL, C. E. "Down Among the Red Men." *Coll Kan State Hist Soc*, XVII (1928), 623-691.

2377 CARRINGTON, Frances Courtney. *My Army Life, and the Fort Phil Kearney Massacre*. Philadelphia, 1910.

2378 CLARK, Joseph Stanley. "Ponca Publicity." *Miss Val Hist Rev*, XXIX (1943), 495-516.

2379 CLUM, John P. "Geronimo." *N M Hist Rev*, III (1928), 1-40, 121-144, 217-264.

2380 CLUM, Woodworth. *Apache Agent: The Story of John P. Clum*. New York, 1936.

2381 CODY, William Frederick. *The Adventures of Buffalo Bill*. New York, 1904.

2382 CODY, William Frederick. *Story of Wild West and Camp Fire Chats*. Philadelphia, 1888.

2383 COLLIER, John C. *The Indians of the Americas*. New York, 1947.†

2384 COOK, James H. *Fifty Years on the Old Frontier*. New Haven, 1923.

2385 COOK, John R. *The Border and the Buffalo*. Topeka, Kan., 1907.

2386 COOLIDGE, Dave, and Mary ROBERTS. *The Navajo Indians*. New York, 1930.

2387 COX, John E. "Soldiering in Dakota Territory in the Seventies: A Communication." *N D Hist Q*, VI (1931), 63-81.

2388 CROOK, George. *General George Crook, His Autobiography*. Norman, Okla., 1946.

2389 CUSTER, Elizabeth Bacon. *Boots and Saddles*. New York, 1885.

2390 CUSTER, Elizabeth Bacon. *Following the Guidon*. New York, 1890.

2391 CUSTER, Elizabeth Bacon. *Tenting on the Plains*. New York, 1895.

2392 CUSTER, George Armstrong. *My Life on the Plains*. New York, 1874.†

2393 DALE, Edward Everett. *The Indians of the Southwest.* Norman, Okla., 1949.

2394 DAVIS, Britton. *The Truth about Geronimo.* New Haven, 1929.

2395 DEBO, Angie. *And Still the Waters Run.* Princeton, 1940.

2396 DEBO, Angie. *A History of the Indians of the United States.* Norman, ￼Okla., 1970.

2397 DE LAND, Charles Edmund. "Sioux Wars." *S D Hist Coll,* XV (1930), 9-730.

2398 DE LAND, Charles Edmund. "The Sioux Wars." *S D Hist Coll,* XVII (1934), 177-551.

2399 DOWNEY, Fairfax David. *Indian-Fighting Army.* New York, 1941.

2400 DRANNAN, William F. *Thirty-One Years on the Plains and in the Mountains.* Chicago, 1900.

2401 DUNN, Jacob Piatt. *Massacres of the Mountains.* New York, 1958.

2402 DUSTIN, Fred. *The Custer Tragedy.* Ann Arbor, 1939.

2403 FARB, Peter. "Rise and Fall of the Indian of the Wild West." *Natl Hist,* LXXVII (1968), 32-41.

2404 FAULK, Odie B. *The Geronimo Campaign.* New York, 1969.

2405 FEE, Chester Anders. *Chief Joseph: The Biography of a Great Indian.* New York, 1936.

2406 FINERTY, John Frederick. *War-Path and Bivouac.* Chicago, 1890.

2407 FORSYTH, George Alexander. *The Story of the Soldier.* New York, 1900.

2408 FRITZ, Henry E. *The Movement for Indian Assimilation, 1860-1890.* Philadelphia, 1963.

2409 GARD, Wayne. *The Great Buffalo Hunt.* New York, 1959.

2410 GARRETSON, Martin S. *A Short History of the American Bison.* New York, 1938.

2411 GERONIMO. *Geronimo's Story of His Life.* New York, 1906.

2412 GITTINGER, Roy. *The Formation of the State of Oklahoma.* Berkeley, 1917.

2413 GRAHAM, William Alexander. *The Story of the Little Big Horn, Custer's Last Fight.* Harrisburg, Pa., 1941.

2414 GRINNELL, George Bird. *The Cheyenne Indians, Their History and Ways of Life.* New Haven, 1923.

2415 GRINNELL, George Bird. *The Fighting Cheyennes.* Norman, Okla., 1956.

2416 HAFEN, Le Roy R., and W. J. GHENT. *Broken Hand: The Life Story of Thomas Fitzpatrick, Chief of the Mountain Men.* Denver, 1931.

2417 HAYTER, Earl W. "The Ponca Removal." *N D Hist Q,* VI (1932), 262-275.

2418 HEBARD, Grace Raymond. *Washakie.* Cleveland, 1930.

2419 HOWARD, Oliver Otis. *My Life and Experiences among Hostile Indians.* Hartford, Conn., 1907.

2420 HYDE, George E. *Red Cloud's Folk: A History of the Oglala Sioux Indians.* Norman, Okla., 1937.

2421 JACKSON, Helen Hunt. *A Century of Dishonor: The Early Crusade for Indian Reform.* New York, 1881.†

2422 JOHNSON, Richard W. *Soldier's Reminiscences in Peace and War.* Philadelphia, 1886.

2423 JOHNSON, Willis Fletcher. *The Red Record of the Sioux.* Philadelphia, 1891.

2424 KING, Charles. *Campaigning with Crook, and Stories of Army Life.* New York, 1890.

2425 LECKIE, William H. *The Buffalo Soldiers: A Narrative of the Negro Cavalry in the West.* Norman, Okla., 1967.

2426 LOCKWOOD, Francis Cummins. *The Apache Indians.* New York, 1938.

2427 MC CRACKEN, Harold. *George Catlin and the Old Frontier.* New York, 1959.

2428 MC LAUGHLIN, James. *My Friend the Indian.* New York, 1910.

2429 MACLEOD, William Christie. *The American-Indian Frontier.* New York, 1928.

2430 MC NICOL, Donald Monroe. *The Amerindians, from Acuera to Sitting Bull, from Donnacona to Big Bear.* New York, 1937.

2431 MANYPENNY, George Washington. *Our Indian Wards.* Cincinnati, 1880.

2432 MAZZANOVICH, Anton. *Trailing Geronimo.* Los Angeles, 1926.

2433 MILES, Nelson Appleton. *The Personal Recollections and Observations of General Nelson A. Miles.* New York, 1896.

2434 MINER, William Harvey. *The American Indians, North of Mexico.* Cambridge, Mass., 1917.

2435 MUNKRES, Robert L. "The Plains Indian Threat on the Oregon Trail." *Ann Wyo,* XL (1968), 193-222.

2436 ODELL, Ruth. *Helen Hunt Jackson.* New York, 1939.

2437 OGLE, Ralph Hedrick. *Federal Control of the Western Apaches, 1848-1886.* Albuquerque, 1940.

2438 OTERO, Miguel Antonio. *My Life on the Frontier.* 2 vols. New York, 1935, 1939.

2439 POOLE, De Witt Clinton. *Among the Sioux of Dakota.* New York, 1881.

2440 PRATT, Richard Henry. *Battlefield and Classroom: Four Decades with the American Indian, 1867-1904.* Ed. Robert M. Utley. New Haven, 1964.

2441 PRIEST, Loring Benson. *Uncle Sam's Stepchildren: The Reformation of United States Indian Policy, 1865-1887.* New Brunswick, 1947.

2442 RADIN, Paul. *The Story of the American Indian.* New York, 1934.

2443 REEVE, Frank D. "The Government and the Navaho, 1883-1888." *N M Hist Rev*, XVIII (1943), 17-51.

2444 RICHARDSON, Rupert Norval. *The Comanche Barrier to South Plains Settlement: A Century and a Half of Savage Resistance to the Advancing White Frontier.* Glendale, Calif., 1933.

2445 RICKEY, Don, Jr. *Forty Miles a Day on Beans and Hay: The Enlisted Soldier Fighting the Indian Wars.* Norman, Okla., 1963.

2446 RISTER, Carl Coke. *Border Command: General Phil Sheridan in the West.* Norman, Okla., 1944.

2447 RISTER, Carl Coke. "The Significance of the Destruction of the Buffalo in the Southwest." *S W Hist Q*, XXXIII (1929), 34-49.

2448 RISTER, Carl Coke. *The Southwestern Frontier, 1865-1881.* Cleveland, 1928.

2449 ROE, Charles Francis. *Custer's Last Battle on the Little Big Horn.* New York, 1927.

2450 ROE, Frank Gilbert. *The Indian and the Horse.* Norman, Okla., 1955.

2451 SANDOZ, Mari. *The Buffalo Hunters: The Story of the Hide Men.* New York, 1954.

2452 SCOTT, Hugh L. *Some Memories of a Soldier.* New York, 1928.

2453 SEYMOUR, Flora Warren. *Indian Agents of the Old Frontier.* New York, 1941.

2454 SEYMOUR, Flora Warren. *The Story of the Red Man.* New York, 1929.

2455 SHIELDS, George O. *The Battle of the Big Hole.* New York, 1889.

2456 STANDING BEAR, Luther. *My People, the Sioux.* Boston and New York, 1928.

2457 STECKMESSER, Kent L. "Custer in Fiction." *Am West*, I (1964), 48-52, 63-64.

2458 SUTLEY, Zachary Taylor. *The Last Frontier.* New York, 1930.

2459 TALLENT, Annie D. *Black Hills: The Last Hunting Ground of the Dakotas.* St. Louis, 1899.

2460 TITUS, Nelson C. "The Last Stand of the Nez Perces." *Wash Hist Q*, VI (1915), 145-153.

2461 TREXLER, H. A. "The Buffalo Range of the Northwest." *Miss Val Hist Rev*, VII (1920), 348-362.

2462 UTLEY, Robert M. *Custer and the Great Controversy: The Origin and Development of a Legend.* Los Angeles, 1962.

2463 UTLEY, Robert M. *The Last Days of the Sioux Nation.* New Haven, 1963.†

2464 VAN DE WATER, Frederic Franklyn. *Glory-Hunter: A Life of General Custer.* New York, 1934.

2465 VAUGHN, J. W. *Indian Fights: New Facts on Seven Encounters.* Norman, Okla., 1966.

2466 VESTAL, Stanley. *Sitting Bull.* Norman, Okla., 1932.

INTELLECTUAL AND CULTURAL CURRENTS

2467 VESTAL, Stanley, ed. *New Sources of Indian History, 1850-1891.* Norman, Okla., 1934.

2468 WALSH, Richard John. *The Making of Buffalo Bill: A Study in Heroics.* Indianapolis, 1928.

2469 WELLMAN, Paul I. *Death in the Desert.* New York, 1935.†

2470 WELLMAN, Paul I. *Death on Horseback; Seventy Years of War for the American West.* Philadelphia, 1947.

2471 WELLMAN, Paul I. *Death on the Prairie.* New York, 1934.†

2472 WHEELER, Homer Webster. *Buffalo Days. Forty Years in the Old West.* Indianapolis, 1925.

2473 WINDOLPH, Charles A. *I Fought with Custer.* New York, 1947.

2474 WISSLER, Clark. *North American Indians of the Plains.* New York, 1920.

XVII. Intellectual and Cultural Currents in American Life

1. General

2475 ADAMS, Henry. *Education.* See 230.†

2476 BEER, Thomas. *The Mauve Decade.* See 320.†

2477 BELLOT, Hugh Hale. *American History and American Historians.* Norman, Okla., 1952.

2478 BOLLER, Paul F. *American Thought in Transition: The Impact of Evolutionary Naturalism, 1865-1900.* See 1798.†

2479 CASE, Victoria, and Robert ORMOND. *We Called It Culture: The Story of Chautauqua.* Garden City, N.Y., 1948.

2480 COMMAGER, Henry S. *The American Mind: An Interpretation of American Thought and Character since the 1880's.* New Haven, 1950.†

2481 CRONIN, Morton. "Currier and Ives: A Content Analysis." *Am Q,* IV (1952), 317-330.

2482 CURTI, Merle. *The Growth of American Thought.* New York, 1964.

2483 DITZION, S. H. *Arsenals of a Democratic Culture: A Social History of the American Public Library Movement in New England and the Middle States, 1850-1900.* Chicago, 1947.

2484 FORBES, Cleon. "St. Louis School of Thought." *Mo Hist Rev,* XXV (1930-1931), 83-101; XXVI (1931), 68-77.

2485 GABRIEL, Ralph Henry. *The Course of American Democratic Thought.* New York, 1956.

2486 GARRATY, John A., ed. *The Transformation of American Society, 1870-1890.* New York, 1968.†

2487 GOULD, Joseph E. *The Chautauqua Movement, An Episode in the Continuing American Revolution.* Albany, 1970.

2488 HALL, G. S. *Life and Confessions of a Psychologist.* New York, 1923.

2489 HART, James D. *The Popular Book: A History of America's Literary Tastes.* New York, 1950.

2490 HERBST, Jurgen. *The German Historical School in American Scholarship: A Study in the Transfer of Culture.* Ithaca, N.Y., 1965.

2491 HOFSTADTER, Richard. *Social Darwinism in American Thought, 1860-1915.* See 1199.†

2492 HUTCHINSON, W. T., ed. *The Marcus W. Jernegan Essays in American Historiography.* Chicago, 1937.

2493 JAMESON, J. F. "American Historical Association." *Am Hist Rev*, XV (1909), 1-20.

2494 KRAUS, Michael. *A History of American History.* New York, 1937.

2495 LYNES, Russell. *The Tastemakers.* New York, 1949.

2496 MILLER,, Perry, ed. *American Thought: Civil War to World War I.* New York, 1954.†

2497 MOTT, Frank Luther. *Golden Multitude: The Story of Best Sellers in the United States.* New York, 1947.

2498 MUMFORD, Lewis. *The Brown Decades.* New York, 1931.†

2499 ODUM, H. W., ed. *American Masters of Social Science.* New York, 1927.

2500 PARRINGTON, Vernon L. *The Beginnings of Critical Realism in America.* Vol. III: *Main Currents in American Thought, 1860-1920.* New York, 1930.

2501 PERSONS, Stow, ed. *Evolutionary Thought in America.* New Haven, 1950.

2502 RESEK, Carl. *Lewis Henry Morgan.* Chicago, 1960.

2503 RILEY, I. W. *American Thought from Puritanism to Pragmatism and Beyond.* New York, 1923.

2504 ROBERTS, Robert. "Gilt, Gingerbread and Realism: The Public and Its Taste." *The Gilded Age: A Reappraisal.* Ed. H. Wayne Morgan. Syracuse, 1963.†

2505 SANBORN, F. B. "Twenty-Five Years." *J Soc Sci*, XXVII (1890), 43-49.

2506 SCHNEIDER, H. W. *History of American Philosophy.* New York, 1946.†

2507 SHEEHAN, Donald. *This Was Publishing: A Chronicle of the Book Trade in the Gilded Age.* Bloomington, 1952.

2508 STERN, B. J. *Lewis Henry Morgan, Social Evolutionist.* Chicago, 1931.

2509 TOWNSEND, H. G. *Philosophical Ideas in United States.* New York, 1934.

2510 WALLACE, Irving. *The Fabulous Showman.* New York, 1959.

2511 WARREN, Austin. "Concord School of Philosophy." *N Eng Q*, II (1929), 199-233.

2512 WISH, Harvey. *Society and Thought in Modern America.* New York, 1952.

2513 ZIFF, Larzer. *The American 1890's: Life and Times of a Lost Generation.* New York, 1966.†

2. Social, Economic, Legal, Philosophical, and Political Thought

2514 BARKER, Charles A. *Henry George.* New York, 1955.

2515 BELLAMY, Edward. *Looking Backward: 2000-1887.* See 1140.†

2516 BELLAMY, Edward. *Talks on Nationalism.* Chicago, 1938.

2517 BUDD, Louis D. *Mark Twain: Social Philosopher.* Bloomington, 1962.

2518 CHUGERMAN, Samuel. *Lester F. Ward: The American Aristotle.* New York, 1965.

2519 CORD, Steven B. *Henry George: Dreamer or Realist.* Philadelphia, 1965.

2520 DIAMOND, William. *The Economic Thought of Woodrow Wilson.* Baltimore, 1934.

2521 DORFMAN, Joseph. *The Economic Mind in American Civilization.* Vol. III. New York, 1949.

2522 DORFMAN, Joseph. *Thorstein Veblen and His America.* New York, 1934.

2523 FINE, Sidney. *Laissez-faire and the General Welfare State.* See 66.†

2524 FRANKLIN, John Hope. "Edward Bellamy and the Nationalist Movement." *N Eng Q*, XI (1938), 739-772.

2525 GEIGER, G. R. *Philosophy of Henry George.* New York, 1933.

2526 GEORGE, Henry. *Progress and Poverty.* New York, 1879.†

2527 GINGER, Ray, ed. *American Social Thought.* New York, 1961.†

2528 GREER, Thomas H. *American Social Reform Movements: Their Pattern since 1865.* New York, 1949.

2529 HARTZ, Louis. *The Liberal Tradition in America: An Interpretation of American Political Thought since the Revolution.* New York, 1955.†

2530 HOFSTADTER, Richard. *Social Darwinism in American Thought.* See 1199.†

2531 HOLMES, Oliver Wendell, Jr. *The Common Law.* Boston, 1881.†

2532 HOOK, Sidney. *John Dewey.* New York, 1939.

2533 HOWE, M. A. De Wolfe. *Justice Holmes: The Proving Years, 1870-1882.* Cambridge, Mass., 1963.

2534 HOWE, M. A. De Wolfe, ed. *Holmes-Laski Letters.* 2 vols. Cambridge, Mass., 1953.†

2535 HOWE, M. A. De Wolfe, ed. *Holmes-Pollock Letters, the Correspondence of Mr. Justice Holmes and Sir Frederick Pollock, 1874-1932.* Cambridge, Mass., 1941.

2536 JAMES, Henry, ed. *The Letters of William James.* 2 vols. Boston, 1920.

2537 JAMES, William. *Pragmatism and Four Essays from the Meaning of Truth.* New York, 1955.†

2538 KELLER, Albert G. *Reminiscences (Mainly Personal) of William Graham Sumner.* New Haven, 1933.

2539 LERNER, Max, ed. *The Mind and Faith of Justice Holmes.* Boston, 1943.

2540 LEWIS, Edward R. *A History of American Political Thought from the Civil War to the World War.* New York, 1937.

2541 MC CLOSKEY, Robert G. *American Conservatism in the Age of Enterprise.* Cambridge, Mass., 1951.†

2542 MANN, Arthur. *Yankee Reformers in the Urban Age.* See 859.

2543 MASON, Alpheus T. *Brandeis: A Free Man's Life.* See 1037.

2544 MATTHIESSEN, F. O. *The James Family, Including Selections from the Writings of Henry James Senior, William, Henry and Alice James.* New York, 1947.

2545 MORGAN, Arthur Ernest. *Edward Bellamy.* New York, 1944.

2546 MORGAN, Arthur Ernest. *The Philosophy of Edward Bellamy.* New York, 1945.

2547 MUMFORD, Lewis. *The Story of Utopias.* New York, 1962.†

2548 PAGE, Charles Hunt. *Class and American Sociology: From Ward to Ross.* New York, 1964.†

2549 PAUL, A. M. *Conservative Crisis and the Rule of Law.* See 1039.†

2550 PERRY, Ralph Barton. *The Thought and Character of William James.* 2 vols. Boston, 1935.

2551 RADER, Benjamin G. *The Academic Mind and Reform: The Influence of Richard T. Ely in American Life.* See 887.

2552 RIESMAN, David. *Thorstein Veblen, a Critical Interpretation.* New York, 1953.

2553 SADLER, Elizabeth. "One Book's Influence, Edward Bellamy's *Looking Backward*." N Eng Q, XVII (1944), 530-555.

2554 SMALL, A. W. *Origins of Sociology.* Chicago, 1924.

2555 VEBLEN, Thorstein.*The Theory of the Leisure Class; an Economic Study in the Evolution of Institutions.* New York, 1899.†

2556 WARD, Lester Frank. *Dynamic Sociology.* New York, 1897.

2557 WARD, Lester Frank. *Psychic Factors in Civilization.* Boston, 1906.

2558 WHITE, Morton G. *Social Thought in America: The Revolt against Formalism.* Boston, 1957.†

2559 WIENER, Philip P. *Evolution and the Founders of Pragmatism.* Cambridge, Mass., 1949.

2560 WILSON, R. Jackson. *In Quest of Community: Social Philosophy in the United States, 1860-1920.* New York, 1968.†

2561 WILSON, Woodrow. *The State.* Boston, 1889, 1898.

2562 YOUNG, A. N. *The Single Tax Movement.* Princeton, 1916.

3. Science and Medicine

2563 AGASSIZ, Alexander. *Letters and Recollections.* Ed. George Agassiz. Boston, 1913.

2564 ARMES, William D., ed. *The Autobiography of Joseph Le Conte.* New York, 1903.

2565 BATES, R. S. *Scientific Societies in the United States.* Cambridge, Mass., 1946.

2566 BOLLER, Paul F., Jr. "New Men and New Ideas: Science and the American Mind." *The Gilded Age: A Reappraisal.* Ed. H. Wayne Morgan. Syracuse, 1963.†

2567 BURBANK, Luther, and Wilbur HALL. *Harvest of Years.* Boston, 1927.

2568 CLARKE, J. M. *James Hall . . . Geologist and Paleontologist.* Albany, 1921.

2569 CUSHING, Harvey. *Life of Sir William Osler.* 2 vols. Oxford, 1925.

2570 DANIELS, George, ed. *Darwinism Comes to America.* Waltham, Mass., 1968.†

2571 DEUTSCH, Albert. *The Mentally Ill in America: A History of Their Care and Treatment from Colonial Times.* Rev. ed. New York, 1946.

2572 DUPREE, A. Hunter. *Science in the Federal Government: A History of Policies and Activities to 1940.* Cambridge, Mass., 1957.

2573 DUPREE, A. Hunter, ed. *Science and the Emergence of Modern America, 1865-1916.* Chicago, 1963.†

2574 EATON, Clement. "Professor James Woodrow and the Freedom of Teaching in the South." See 1815.

2575 FISKE, John. *Century of Science.* Boston, 1899.

2576 FISKE, John. *The Destiny of Man.* Boston, 1884, 1912.

2577 FISKE, T. S. "Mathematical Progress." *Sci,* XXI (1905), 209-215.

2578 FLEMING, Donald. *John William Draper and the Religion of Science.* Philadelphia, 1950.

2579 FLEMING, Donald. *William H. Welch and the Rise of Modern Medicine.* Boston, 1954.

2580 FLEXNER, Simon, and J. T. FLEXNER. *William Henry Welch and the Heroic Age of American Medicine.* New York, 1941.

2581 GILMAN, Daniel Coit. *The Life of James Dwight Dana.* New York, 1899.

2582 GOODE, G. B., ed. *Smithsonian Institution.* Washington, D.C., 1897.

2583 GRAY, Asa. *Darwiniana.* New York, 1876, 1899.†

2584 HOLDEN, E. S. "Achievements in Astronomy." *Forum,* XV (1893), 744-752.

2585 JAFFE, Bernard. *Men of Science in America. The Role of Science in the Growth of Our Country.* New York, 1944.

2586 JORDAN, D. S., ed. *Leading American Men of Science.* New York, 1910.

2587 LOEWENBERG, B. J. "Darwinism Comes to America." *Miss Val Hist Rev,* XXVIII (1940), 339-368.

2588 LOEWENBERG, B. J. "Reaction of American Scientists to Darwinism." *Am Hist Rev,* XXXVIII (1933), 687-701.

2589 MC GEE, W. J. "Fifty Years of American Science." *Atl Month,* LXXXII (1898), 307-320.

2590 MILLER, Howard S. *Dollars for Research: Science and Its Patrons in Nineteenth Century America.* Seattle, 1970.

2591 NEWCOMB, Simon. "Recent Astronomical Progress." *Forum,* XXV (1898), 109-119.

2592 NEWCOMB, Simon. *The Reminiscences of an Astronomer.* Boston, 1903.

2593 OSBORN, H. F. *Cope, Master Naturalist.* Princeton, 1931.

2594 PACKARD, F. R. *History of Medicine in the United States.* 2 vols. New York, 1931.

2595 RATNER, Sidney. "Evolution and Rise of Scientific Spirit." *Philos Sci,* III (1936), 104-122.

2596 ROBERTS, Mary M. *American Nursing: History and Interpretation.* New York, 1954.

2597 RUKEYSER, Muriel. *Willard Gibbs.* Garden City, N.Y., 1942.

2598 SCHUCHERT, Charles, and Clare Mae LEVINE. *O. C. Marsh: Pioneer in Paleontology.* New Haven, 1940.

2599 SHALER, N. S. *Autobiography . . . with a Supplementary Memoir by His Wife.* Boston, 1909.

2600 SHRADY, G. F. "Recent Triumphs in Medicine and Surgery." *Forum,* XXIII (1897), 28-41.

2601 SHRYOCK, Richard H. *American Medical Research.* New York, 1947.

2602 SHRYOCK, Richard H. *The Development of Modern Medicine.* New York, 1947.

2603 SIGERIST, H. E. *American Medicine.* New York, 1934.

2604 SMITH, H. N. "King, Powell, and Establishment of Geological Survey." *Miss Val Hist Rev,* XXXIV (1947), 37-58.

2605 TAYLOR, J. A. *History of Dentistry.* Philadelphia and New York, 1922.

2606 TOBEY, James A. *The National Government and Public Health.* Baltimore, 1926.

2607 WHITE, Edward A. *Science and Religion in American Thought.* See 1871.

2608 WILLIAMS, H. S. *Luther Burbank, His Life and Work.* New York, 1915.

2609 WILSON, R. J., ed. *Darwinism and the American Intellectual.* Homewood, Ill., 1967.†

4. Letters

2610 ADAMS, Richard P. "Southern Literature in the 1890's." *Miss Q*, XXI (1968), 277-281.

2611 AHNEBRINK, Lars. *The Beginning of Naturalism in American Fiction: A Study of the Works of Hamlin Garland, Stephen Crane and Frank Norris with Special Reference to Some European Influences, 1891-1903.* Cambridge, Mass., 1950.

2612 BARNETT, James H. *Divorce and the American Divorce Novel, 1858-1937.* Philadelphia, 1939.

2613 BEER, Thomas. *Stephen Crane: A Study in American Letters.* Garden City, N.Y., 1923.

2614 BELLAMY, G. C. *Mark Twain as Literary Artist.* Norman, Okla., 1950.

2615 BERRYMAN, John. *Stephen Crane.* New York, 1950.†

2616 BERTHOFF, Werner. *The Ferment of Realism: American Literature, 1884-1919.* New York, 1966.

2617 BLAIR, Walter. *Mark Twain and Huck Finn.* Berkeley, 1960.

2618 BONE, Robert A. *The Negro Novel in America.* Rev. ed. New Haven, 1965.†

2619 BROOKS, Van Wyck. *The Confident Years, 1885-1915.* New York, 1952.

2620 BROOKS, Van Wyck. *Howells, His Life and World.* New York, 1959.

2621 BROOKS, Van Wyck. *New England: Indian Summer, 1865-1915.* New York, 1940.†

2622 BROOKS, Van Wyck. *The Ordeal of Mark Twain.* Rev. ed. New York, 1933.†

2623 BRUCE, Franklin H. *Future Perfect; American Science Fiction of the Nineteenth Century.* New York, 1966.

2624 BUCKINGHAM, Willis J., ed. *Emily Dickinson, an Annotated Bibliography; Writings, Scholarship, Criticism, and Ana.* Bloomington, 1970.

2625 CADY, Edwin Harrison. *The Realist at War; the Mature Years, 1885-1920, of William Dean Howells.* Syracuse, 1958.

2626 CADY, Edwin Harrison. *The Road to Realism; the Early Years, 1837-1885, of William Dean Howells.* Syracuse, 1956.

2627 CANBY, H. S. *Walt Whitman.* Boston, 1943.

2628 CARTER, Everett. *Howells and the Age of Realism.* Philadelphia, 1954.

2629 COOKE, D. G. *William Dean Howells: A Critical Study.* New York, 1922.

2630 DE VOTO, Bernard. *Mark Twain's America.* Boston, 1932.†

2631 DE VOTO, Bernard, ed. *Mark Twain in Eruption.* New York, 1940.†

2632 DUPEE, Frederick Wilcox. *Henry James.* New York, 1951.

2633 ELIAS, Robert Henry. *Theodore Dreiser, Apostle of Nature.* New York, 1949.

2634 FALK, Robert. "The Search for Reality: Writers and Their Literature." *The Gilded Age: A Reappraisal.* Ed. H. Wayne Morgan. Syracuse, 1963.†

2635 FALK, Robert. *The Victorian Mode in American Fiction, 1865-1885.* East Lansing, Mich., 1965.

2636 FONER, Philip Sheldon. *Jack London, American Rebel.* New York, 1947.†

2637 FORBES, Allyn B. "The Literary Quest for Utopia." *Soc Forces*, VI (1927), 179-189.

2638 GEISMAR, Maxwell David, *Mark Twain: An American Prophet.* Boston, 1971.

2639 GEISMAR, Maxwell David. *Rebels and Ancestors: The American Novel, 1890-1915.* Boston, 1953.†

2640 HALL, Wade. *The Smiling Phoenix: Southern Humor from 1865 to 1910.* Gainesville, Fla., 1965.

2641 HERBST, Jurgen. *The German Historical School in American Scholarship.* See 2490.

2642 HICKS, Granville. *The Great Tradition: An Interpretation of American Literature since the Civil War.* New York, 1935.†

2643 HOWELLS, William Dean. *Life in Letters.* Ed. Mildred Howells. 2 vols. New York, 1928.

2644 HOWELLS, William Dean. *Literary Friends and Acquaintances.* New York, 1900.†

2645 HOWELLS, William Dean. *Literary Passions.* New York, 1895.

2646 KAPLAN, Justin. *Mr. Clemens and Mark Twain. A Biography.* New York, 1966.†

2647 KAZIN, Alfred. *On Native Ground.* New York, 1942.†

2648 KAZIN, Alfred, and Charles SHAPIRO, eds. *The Stature of Theodore Dreiser: A Critical Survey of the Man and His Work.* Bloomington, 1955.†

2649 LUBBOCK, Percy, ed. *Letters of Henry James.* 2 vols. New York, 1920.

2650 LYNN, Kenneth. *The Dream of Success: A Study of the Modern American Imagination.* Boston, 1955.

2651 MARTIN, Jay. *Harvests of Change: American Literature, 1865-1914.* New York, 1967.†

2652 MATTHIESSEN, F. O. *Henry James: The Major Phase.* New York, 1944.†

2653 MATTHIESSEN, F. O. *The James Family.* See 2544.

2654 MATTHIESSEN, F. O. *Theodore Dreiser.* New York, 1951.

2655 MATTHIESSEN, F. O., and K. B. MURDOCK, eds. *The Notebooks of Henry James.* New York, 1947.†

2656 MORGAN, H. Wayne. *American Writers in Rebellion: From Mark Twain to Dreiser.* New York, 1965.†

2657 NEIDER, Charles. *The Autobiography of Mark Twain.* New York, 1959.

2658 PAINE, Albert Bigelow, ed. *Mark Twain's Letters, Arranged with Comment.* 2 vols. New York, 1917.

2659 PATTEE, F. L. *American Literature since 1870.* New York, 1915.

2660 PATTEE, F. L. *Development of Short Story.* New York, 1923.

2661 PEARSON, E. L. *Dime Novels.* Boston, 1929.

2662 PERRY, Bliss. *Walt Whitman: His Life and Work.* Boston, 1906.

2663 PIZER, Donald. "Late Nineteenth Century American Realism: An Essay in Definition." *N C F,* XVI (1961), 263-269.

2664 PIZER, Donald. *Realism and Naturalism in Nineteenth Century American Literature.* Carbondale, Ill., 1966.

2665 SHURTER, Robert L. "The Utopian Novel in America, 1888-1900." *S Atl Q,* XXIV (1935), 137-144.

2666 SMITH, Henry Nash. *Mark Twain: The Development of a Writer.* Cambridge, Mass., 1962.†

2667 SMITH, Henry Nash, and William M. GIBSON, eds. *Mark Twain-Howells Letters: The Correspondence of Samuel Clemens and William D. Howells, 1872-1910.* Cambridge, Mass., 1960.

2668 SPILLER, Robert E. *The Cycle of American Literature.* New York, 1955.†

2669 SPILLER, Robert E., et al., eds. *Literary History of the United States.* Rev. ed. New York, 1963.

2670 TAGGARD, Genevieve. *Emily Dickinson.* New York, 1930.

2671 TAYLOR, Walter F. *The Economic Novel in America* [*1865-1900*]. Chapel Hill, 1942.

2672 TICKNOR, Caroline. *Glimpses of Authors.* Boston, 1924.

2673 TRAUBEL, H. L. *With Walt Whitman in Camden.* 3 vols. Boston and New York, 1904-1906.

2674 TURNER, Arlin. *George W. Cable: A Biography.* Durham, N.C., 1956.†

2675 VANDERBILT, Kermit. *The Achievement of William Dean Howells: A Reinterpretation.* Princeton, 1968.

2676 VAN DOREN, Carl. *The American Novel, 1789-1939.* New York, 1940.

2677 WAGENKNECHT, Edward C. *Cavalcade of American Novel.* New York, 1952.

2678 WAGENKNECHT, Edward C. *William Dean Howells: The Friendly Eye.* New York, 1969.

2679 WALLACE, Lew. *An Autobiography.* 2 vols. New York, 1906.

2680 WESTBROOK, Percy D. *Acres of Flint: Writers of Rural New England, 1870-1900.* Washington, D.C., 1951.

2681 WILSON, Edmund. *The Shock of Recognition: The Development of Literature in the United States Recorded by the Men Who Made It.* New York, 1955.

5. Education

2682 BARKER, J. M. *Colleges in America.* Cleveland, 1894.

2683 BARNARD, John. *From Evangelicanism to Progressivism at Oberlin College, 1866-1917.* Columbus, Ohio, 1969.

2684 BATES, R. S. *Scientific Societies in the United States.* See 2565.

2685 BEALE, Howard K. *Are American Teachers Free?* New York, 1936.

2686 BECK, Holmes. "American Progressive Education, 1875-1930." Doctoral dissertation, Yale University, 1941.

2687 BOONE, R. G. *Education in the United States.* New York, 1894.

2688 BRYCE, James. "American College." *Atl Month,* LXXXV (1895), 703-706.

2689 BURNS, J. A., et al. *History of Catholic Education.* New York, 1937.

2690 BUTTS, R. Freeman, and Lawrence A. CREMIN. *A History of Education in American Culture.* New York, 1953.

2691 CREMIN, Lawrence A. *The Transformation of the School: Progressivism in American Education.* New York, 1961.†

2692 CUBBERLEY, Ellwood P. *Public Education in the United States.* Boston, 1919.

2693 CUNNINGHAM, E. R. "Medical Education."

2694 CURTI, Merle. *The Social Ideas of American Educators.* New York, 1935.†

2695 CURTI, Merle, and Vernon CARSTENSEN. *The University of Wisconsin: A History, 1848-1925.* Madison, 1949.

2696 DABNEY, Charles William. *Universal Education in the South.* 2 vols. Chapel Hill, 1936.

2697 DEXTER, E. G. *Education in the United States.* New York, 1904.

2698 ELY, R. T. "American Economic Association." *Pub Am Econ Assoc,* XI (1910), 47-93.

2699 FERNBERGER, S. W. "American Psychological Association." *Psych Bull,* XXIX (1932), 1-89.

2700 FLEXNER, Abraham. *Gilman.* New York, 1946.

2701 FRANKLIN, Fabian. *The Life of Daniel Coit Gilman.* New York, 1910.

2702 FRENCH, John C. *A History of the University Founded by Johns Hopkins.* Baltimore, 1946.

2703 GILMAN, Daniel Coit. *The Launching of a University.* New York, 1906.

2704 GILMAN, Daniel Coit. *University Problems*. New York, 1898.

2705 GOODSPEED, T. W. *William Rainey Harper*. Chicago, 1928.

2706 HALL, G. S. "Social Life in Colleges." *Lippincott's*, XXXIX-XL (1887-1888), 152-163, 572-578, 677-687, 737-743, 999-1007.

2707 HALL, G. S. "Student Customs." *Proc Am Ant Soc*, XIV (1900-1901), 83-124.

2708 HALL, G. S. "Undergraduate Life." *Scrib Mag*, XXI-XXII (1897), 3-29, 531-555, 663-691.

2709 HAWKINS, Hugh. "Charles W. Eliot, University Reform and Religious Faith in America, 1869-1909." *J Am Hist*, LI (1964), 191-213.

2710 HAWKINS, Hugh. *Pioneer: A History of the Johns Hopkins University*. Ithaca, N.Y., 1960.

2711 HERBST, Jurgen. *The German Historical School in American Scholarship*. See 2490.

2712 HOFSTADTER, Richard, and Walter P. METZGER. *The Development of Academic Freedom in the United States*. New York, 1955.

2713 HOFSTADTER, Richard, and Wilson SMITH. *American Higher Education: A Documentary History*. 2 vols. Chicago, 1961.†

2714 HOLT, W. Stull, ed. *Historical Scholarship in the United States, 1876-1901: As Revealed in the Correspondence of Herbert B. Adams*. Baltimore, 1938.

2715 HOOK, Sidney. *John Dewey*. See 2532.

2716 JAMES, Henry, III. *Charles W. Eliot, President of Harvard University, 1869-1909*. 2 vols. Boston, 1930.

2717 KLEMM, R. L. "Legal Education." *Rep U S Comm Ed*, II (1890-1891), 376-445.

2718 KNIGHT, Edgar Wallace. *Education in the United States*. Boston, 1951.

2719 KNIGHT, Edgar Wallace. *Public Education in the South*. Boston, 1922.

2720 KRUG, Edward A. *The Shaping of the American High School: 1880-1920*. Madison, 1969.

2721 KRUG, Edward A., ed. *Charles W. Eliot on Education*. New York, 1962.†

2722 MANLEY, Robert. *Centennial History of the University of Nebraska*. Vol. I: *Frontier University, 1869-1919*. Lincoln, Neb., 1969.

2723 MINNICH, Harvey C. *William Holmes McGuffey and His Readers*. New York, 1936.

2724 MORISON, Samuel Eliot. *The Development of Harvard University since the Inauguration of President Eliot, 1869-1929*. Cambridge, Mass., 1930.

2725 MOSIER, Richard D. *Making the American Mind: Social and Moral Ideas in the McGuffey Readers*. New York, 1947.

2726 PARSONS, Kermit Carlyle. *The Cornell Campus: A History of Its Planning and Development*. Ithaca, N.Y., 1969.

2727 PIERSON, George Wilson. *Yale College: An Educational History, 1871-1921*. New Haven, 1952.

2728 REISNER, E. H. *Evolution of the Common School.* New York, 1930.

2729 ROSS, Earl Dudley. *Democracy's College.* Ames, Iowa, 1942.

2730 SCHMIDT, George P. *The Liberal Arts College: A Chapter in American Cultural History.* New Brunswick, 1957.

2731 SEARS, J. B. *Philanthrophy in Higher Education.* Washington, D.C., 1922.

2732 SERVIN, Manuel, and Wilson Iris HIGBIE. *Southern California and Its University: A History of U.S.C. (1880-1964).* Los Angeles, 1969.

2733 SHELDON, H. D. *Student Life and Customs.* New York, 1901.

2734 SIZER, Theodore R. *Secondary Schools at the Turn of the Century.* New Haven, 1964.

2735 STORR, Richard J. *Harper's University: The Beginnings. A History of the University of Chicago.* Chicago, 1966.

2736 THWING, C. F. *Education since the Civil War.* Boston, 1910.

2737 THWING, C. F. *Higher Education in America.* New York, 1906.

2738 TRUE, A. C. "Agricultural Education." *Yrbk Dept of Ag* (1889), 157-190.

2739 VAN TASSEL, David D. "The American Historical Association and the South, 1884-1913." *J S Hist,* XXIII (1957), 465-482.

2740 VEBLEN, Thorstein. *Higher Learning in America.* New York, 1918.†

2741 VEYSEY, Laurence R. *The Emergence of the American University.* Chicago, 1965.†

2742 WELTER, Rush. *Popular Education and Democratic Thought in America.* New York, 1963.

2743 WHITE, Andrew D. *Autobiography of Andrew Dickson White.* 2 vols. New York, 1905.

2744 WILLIAMS, Howard. *A History of Colgate University (1819-1969).* New York, 1969.

2745 WILLOUGHBY, W. W. "Summer Schools." *Rep U S Comm Ed,* II (1891-1892), 893-959.

2746 WOODY, Thomas. *A History of Women's Education in the United States.* New York, 1929.

6. Journalism

2747 BAEHR, J. W., Jr. *The* New York Tribune *since the Civil War.* New York, 1936.

2748 BARRETT, James Wyman. *Joseph Pulitzer and His World.* New York, 1941.

2749 BAUMGARTNER, Appolinaris W. *Catholic Journalism: A Study of Its Development in the United States, 1789-1930.* New York, 1931.

2750 BERGER, Meyer. *The Story of the* New York Times. New York, 1951.

2751 BLEYER, Willard G. *Main Currents in the History of Journalism*. New York, 1927.

2752 BOK, Edward William. *The Americanization of Edward Bok*. New York, 1920.

2753 BRITT, George. *Forty Years—Forty Millions: The Career of Frank A. Munsey*. New York, 1935.

2754 CLARK, Thomas D. *The Southern Country Editor*. See 2055.

2755 CLINE, H. F. "B. O. Flower and the Arena." *Jour Q*, XVII (1940), 139-150, 171, 247-257.

2756 CORTISSOZ, Royal. *The New York Tribune*. New York, 1923.

2757 DABNEY, Thomas E. *One Hundred Great Years: The Story of the* Times-Picayune *from Its Founding to 1940*. Baton Rouge, 1944.

2758 DANIELS, Josephus. *Editor in Politics*. Chapel Hill, 1941.

2759 DANIELS, Josephus. *Tar Heel Editor*. Chapel Hill, 1939.

2760 DILL, W. A. *Growth of Newspapers in the United States, 1704-1925*. Lawrence, Kan., 1928.

2761 DUNNE, Finley Peter. *Mr. Dooley's Opinions*. New York, 1901.

2762 ELLIS, Elmer. *Mr. Dooley's America: A Life of Finley Peter Dunne*. New York, 1941.

2763 GILDER, Richard Watson. *Letters*. New York, 1916.

2764 GODKIN, E. L. *Reflections and Comments*. See 259.

2765 GRAMLING, Oliver. *AP, the Story of News*. New York, 1940.

2766 GRIMES, Alan P. *Political Liberalism of the New York Nation, 1865-1932*. New York, 1953.†

2767 HENDRICK, B. J. *Life and Letters of Walter Hines Page*. 3 vols. Garden City, N.Y., 1922-1925.

2768 HOOKER, Richard. *The Story of an Independent Newspaper* [Springfield Republican]. New York, 1924.

2769 HOWE, M. A. De Wolfe. *The* Atlantic Monthly. Boston, 1919.

2770 JOHNSON, Walter. *William Allen White's America*. New York, 1947.

2771 JUERGENS, George. *Joseph Pulitzer and the* New York World. Princeton, 1966.

2772 KINSLEY, Philip. *The* Chicago Tribune, *Its First Hundred Years*. 3 vols. New York, 1943-1946.

2773 LEE, James Melvin. *History of American Journalism*. Boston, 1923.

2774 LUTZKY, Seymour. "The Reform Editors and Their Press." Doctoral dissertation, State University of Iowa, 1951.

2775 LYON, Peter. *Success Story: The Life and Times of S. S. McClure*. New York, 1963.

2776 MC CLURE, S. S. *My Autobiography*. See 278.

2777 MC RAE, M. A. *Forty Years in Newspaperdom.* New York, 1924.

2778 MITCHELL, Edward P. *Memoirs of an Editor: Fifty Years of American Journalism.* New York, 1924.

2779 MOTT, Frank Luther. *American Journalism.* New York, 1941.

2780 MOTT, Frank Luther. *A History of American Magazines, 1885-1905.* Cambridge, Mass., 1957.

2781 NEVINS, Allan. *The* Evening Post. New York, 1922.

2782 NIXON, Raymond B. *Henry B. Grady, Spokesman of the New South.* See 2071.

2783 OGDEN, Rollo. *Life and Letters of Godkin.* See 189.

2784 PAINE, A. B. *Thomas Nast.* See 193.

2785 RAMMELKAMP, Julian S. *Pulitzer's* Post-Dispatch, *1878-1883.* Princeton, 1967.

2786 ROSEBAULT, C. J. *When Dana Was the* Sun. New York, 1931.

2787 ROSEWATER, Victor. *History of Cooperative News-Gathering in the United States.* New York, 1930.

2788 SEITZ, Don C. *Joseph Pulitzer: His Life and Letters.* New York, 1924.

2789 SHAW, Archer Hayes. *The* Plain Dealer, *One Hundred Years in Cleveland.* New York, 1942.

2790 STACKPOLE, Edward J. *Behind the Scenes with a Newspaper Man: Fifty Years in the Life of an Editor.* Philadelphia, 1927.

2791 STONE, Cadance. *Dana and the* Sun. New York, 1938.

2792 STONE, M. E. *Fifty Years a Journalist.* New York, 1921.

2793 SWANBERG, W. A. *Citizen Hearst.* New York, 1961.

2794 THORNBROUGH, Emma Lou. "American Negro Newspapers, 1880-1914." See 1981.

2795 WALL, Joseph F. *Henry Watterson.* See 219.

2796 WARD, W. H. "Fifty Years of *Independent.*" *Independent,* L (1898), 1642-1646.

2797 WATTERSON, Henry. "Marse Henry." See 308.

2798 WEISBERGER, Bernard A. *The American Newspaperman.* Chicago, 1961.

2799 WHITE, William Allen. *The Autobiography of William Allen White.* See 311.

2800 WILSON, James H. *The Life of Charles A. Dana.* New York, 1907.

7. Painting and Sculpting

2801 CAFFIN, C. H. *American Painting.* London, 1907.

2802 CORTISSOZ, Royal. *American Artists.* New York, 1923.

2803 GARRETT, Wendell D., et al. *The Arts in America: The Nineteenth Century.* New York, 1969.

2804 GOODRICH, Lloyd. *Albert P. Ryder.* New York, 1959.

2805 GOODRICH, Lloyd. *Thomas Eakins: His Life and Work.* New York, 1933.

2806 GOODRICH, Lloyd. *Winslow Homer.* New York, 1945.

2807 ISHAM, Samuel. *The History of American Painting.* New ed. New York, 1927.

2808 LARKIN, Oliver W. *Art and Life in America.* New York, 1949.

2809 MC SPADDEN, J. W. *Famous Sculptors of America.* New York, 1924.

2810 MATHER, F. J., et al. *American Spirit in Art.* New York, 1927.

2811 NEUHAUS, Eugene. *American Art.* Stanford, 1931.

2812 PENNELL, Elizabeth Robins, and Joseph PENNELL. *The Life of James McNeill Whistler.* Philadelphia, 1908.

2813 PRICE, Frederic Newlin. *Ryder.* New York, 1932.

2814 SAINT-GAUDENS, Augustus. *Reminiscences.* Ed. Homer Saint-Gaudens. 2 vols. New York, 1913.

2815 THORP, Louise Hall. *Saint-Gaudens and the Gilded Era.* Boston, 1969.

8. Architecture

2816 ANDREWS, Wayne. *Architecture, Ambition, and Americans.* New York, 1955.†

2817 BALDWIN, C. C. *Stanford White.* New York, 1931.

2818 BURCHARD, John, and Albert BUSH-BROWN. *The Architecture of America: A Social and Cultural History.* Boston, 1961.†

2819 CONDIT, Carl W. *American Building Art: The Nineteenth Century.* New York, 1961.

2820 CONDIT, Carl W. *The Rise of the Skyscraper.* Chicago, 1952.

2821 FITCH, James Marston. *Architecture and the Esthetics of Plenty.* New York, 1961.

2822 GIBSON, L. H. *Beautiful Houses.* New York, 1895.

2823 GIBSON, L. H. *Convenient Houses.* New York, 1889.

2824 HAMLIN, T. F. *The American Spirit in Architecture.* New Haven, 1926.

2825 HITCHCOCK, Henry Russell, Jr. *The Architecture of H. H. Richardson and His Times.* New York, 1936.†

2826 HITCHCOCK, Henry Russell, Jr. *In the Nature of Materials, 1887-1941: The Buildings of Frank Lloyd Wright.* New York, 1942.

2827 LARKIN, Oliver W. *Art and Life in America.* See 2808.

2828 MOORE, Charles. *The Life and Times of Charles Follen McKim.* Boston, 1929.

2829 MORRISON, Hugh S. *Louis Sullivan: Prophet of Modern Architecture.* New York, 1935.†

2830 MUMFORD, Lewis. *The Brown Decades.* See 2498.†

2831 MUMFORD, Lewis. Sticks and Stones. New York, 1924.†

2832 SCHUYLER, Montgomery. *American Architecture.* New York, 1892.†

2833 STEINMAN, D. B. *The Builders of the Bridge: The Story of John Roebling and His Son.* New York, 1950.

2834 TALLMADGE, T. E. *The Story of Architecture in America.* Rev. ed. New York, 1936.

2835 TUNNARD, Christopher, and Henry Hope REED. *American Skyline: The Growth and Form of Our Cities and Towns.* Boston, 1955.†

9. Music and Theater

2836 CHASE, Gilbert. *America's Music.* Rev. ed. New York, 1966.

2837 COAD, O. S., and Edwin MIMS. *The American Stage.* New Haven, 1929.

2838 CULSHAW, John. *A Century of Music.* London, 1952.

2839 DAMROSCH, Walter. *My Musical Life.* New York, 1923.

2840 DE KOVEN, Anna. *Musician and His Wife.* New York, 1926.

2841 DREW, John. *My Years on the Stage.* New York, 1922.

2842 GILBERT, Douglas. *American Vaudeville.* New York, 1940.†

2843 GRAU, Robert. *Forty Years' Observation of Music and Drama.* New York, 1909.

2844 GROSSMAN, E. B. *Edwin Booth.* Union Square, N.Y., 1894.

2845 HIPSHER, E. E. *American Opera and Its Composers.* Philadelphia, 1934.

2846 HORNBLOW, Arthur. *A History of the Theater in America.* 2 vols. Philadelphia, 1919.

2847 HOWARD, John Tasker. *Our American Music.* Rev. ed. New York, 1946.

2848 HOWE, M. A. De Wolfe. *The Boston Symphony Orchestra.* Boston, 1931.

2849 JEFFERSON, Joseph. *Autobiography.* New York, 1890.

2850 LAHEE, H. C. *Grand Opera in America.* Boston, 1902.

2851 MC KAY, F. E., and C. E. L. WINGATE, eds. *Famous American Actors.* New York, 1896.

2852 QUINN, A. H. *American Drama from the Civil War.* New York, 1936.

2853 SKINNER, Otis. *Footlights and Spotlights.* Indianapolis, 1924.

2854 SMITH, H. B. *First Nights and First Editions.* Boston, 1931.

2855 SOBEL, Bernard. *Burleycue.* New York, 1931.

2856 SPAETH, Sigmund G. *A History of Popular Music in America.* New York, 1948.

2857 STRANG, L. C. *Celebrated Comedians of Light Opera.* Boston, 1901.

2858 STRANG, L. C. *Famous Actors of the Day.* Boston, 1899.

2859 STRANG, L. C. *Famous Actresses of the Day.* Boston, 1901.

2860 STRANG, L. C. *Players and Plays of Last Quarter Century.* Boston, 1902.

2861 STRANG, L. C. *Prima Donnas and Soubrettes of Light Opera.* Boston, 1900.

2862 THOMAS, Theodore. *A Musical Autobiography.* 2 vols. Chicago, 1905.

2863 TOWSE, J. R. *Sixty Years of Theater.* New York, 1916.

2864 UPTON, G. P. *Musical Memories.* Chicago, 1908.

2865 WINTER, William. *Life and Art of Joseph Jefferson.* New York, 1894.

Addenda

III. American Politics from Rutherford B. Hayes to Grover Cleveland, 1877–1897

2. Biographies

2866 DAVISON, Kenneth E. *The Presidency of Rutherford B. Hayes.* Westport, Conn., 1972.

2867 KOENIG, Louis W. *A Political Biography of William Jennings Bryan.* New York, 1972.

4. From Hayes to Cleveland, 1877–1897

2868 DAVISON, Kenneth E. *Presidency of Hayes.* See 2869.

2869 MARCUS, Robert D. *Grand Old Party: Political Structure in the Gilded Age, 1880–1896.* New York, 1971.

VI. State and Local Politics

2870 BARR, Alwyn. *Reconstruction to Reform: Texas Politics, 1876–1906.* Austin, 1971.

2871 MABRY, William A. *The Negro in North Carolina Politics Since Reconstruction.* Durham, N.C., 1940.

2872 MABRY, William A. "Negro Suffrage and Fusion Rule in North Carolina." *N C Hist Rev,* XII (1935), 79–102.

2873 UZEE, Philip D. "The Republican Party in the Louisiana Election of 1896." *La Hist,* II (1961), 332–344.

VIII. Constitutional Developments

2874 FRANKFURTER, Felix. *The Commerce Clause Under Marshall, Tainey, and Waite.* Chapel Hill, 1937.

2875 LEVY, Leonard W. *American Constitutional Law: Historical Essays.* New York, 1966.

XIII. The Rise of Industry

1. General

2876 BOLLER, Paul F. *American Thought in Transition: The Impact of Evolutionary Nationalism, 1865-1900.* New York, 1969.

2877 JONES, Howard Mumford. *The Age of Energy: Varieties of American Experience, 1865-1915.* New York, 1971.

2878 WALKER, Robert H. *Life in the Age of Enterprise, 1865-1900.* New York, 1971.

XIV. America in the Gilded Age

2. Immigration

2879 DUNNE, Thomas, and William TIFFT. *Ellis Island.* New York, 1971.

2880 ESSLINGER, Dean R. "The Urbanization of South Bend Immigrants, 1850-1880." Doctoral dissertation, University of Notre Dame, 1972.

2881 WHEELER, Thomas C., ed. *The Anguish of Becoming American.* New York, 1971.

5. Religion

2882 CARTER, Paul A. *The Spiritual Crisis of the Gilded Age.* De Kalb, Ill., 1972.

6. The Negro

2883 FREDERICKSON, George M. *The Black Image in the White Mind: The Debate on Afro-American Character and Destiny, 1817-1914.* New York, 1971.

2884 MABRY, William A. *The Negro in North Carolina Politics Since Reconstruction.* See 2871.

2885 MABRY, William A. "Negro Suffrage and Fusion Rule in North Carolina." See 2872.

2886 MEIER, August. "The Negro and the Democratic Party, 1875-1915." *Phylon,* XVII (1956), 185-188.

XVII. Intellectual and Cultural Currents in American Life

1. General

2887 HALE, Nathan, Jr. *The Beginnings of Psychoanalysis in the United States, 1876-1917.* New York, 1971.

NOTES

INDEX

INDEX

INDEX

INDEX

INDEX

INDEX

INDEX

INDEX

INDEX

INDEX

INDEX

INDEX

P—R

INDEX

INDEX

S

INDEX

INDEX

INDEX